PEARL HARBOR
FACT AND REFERENCE BOOK
EVERYTHING TO KNOW ABOUT DECEMBER 7, 1941

PEARL HARBOR
FACT AND REFERENCE BOOK
EVERYTHING TO KNOW ABOUT DECEMBER 7, 1941

By Terence McComas

MUTUAL PUBLISHING

Copyright ©1991 by Mutual Publishing

Design
Michael Horton Design

Imagesetting & Typesetting
PrintPrep Of Hawaii

Photos
Hawaii State Archives
National Archives

All rights reserved

No part of this book may be reproduced in any form or by any electronic or mechanical means including information storage and retrieval devices or systems without prior written permission from the publisher except that brief passages may be quoted for interviews.

First Printing November 1991
123456789

ISBN#0-935180-02-8

Mutual Publishing
1127 11th Avenue
Honolulu, Hawaii 96816
Telephone (808) 732-1709
Fax (808) 734-4094

For
Camille and "Spud"

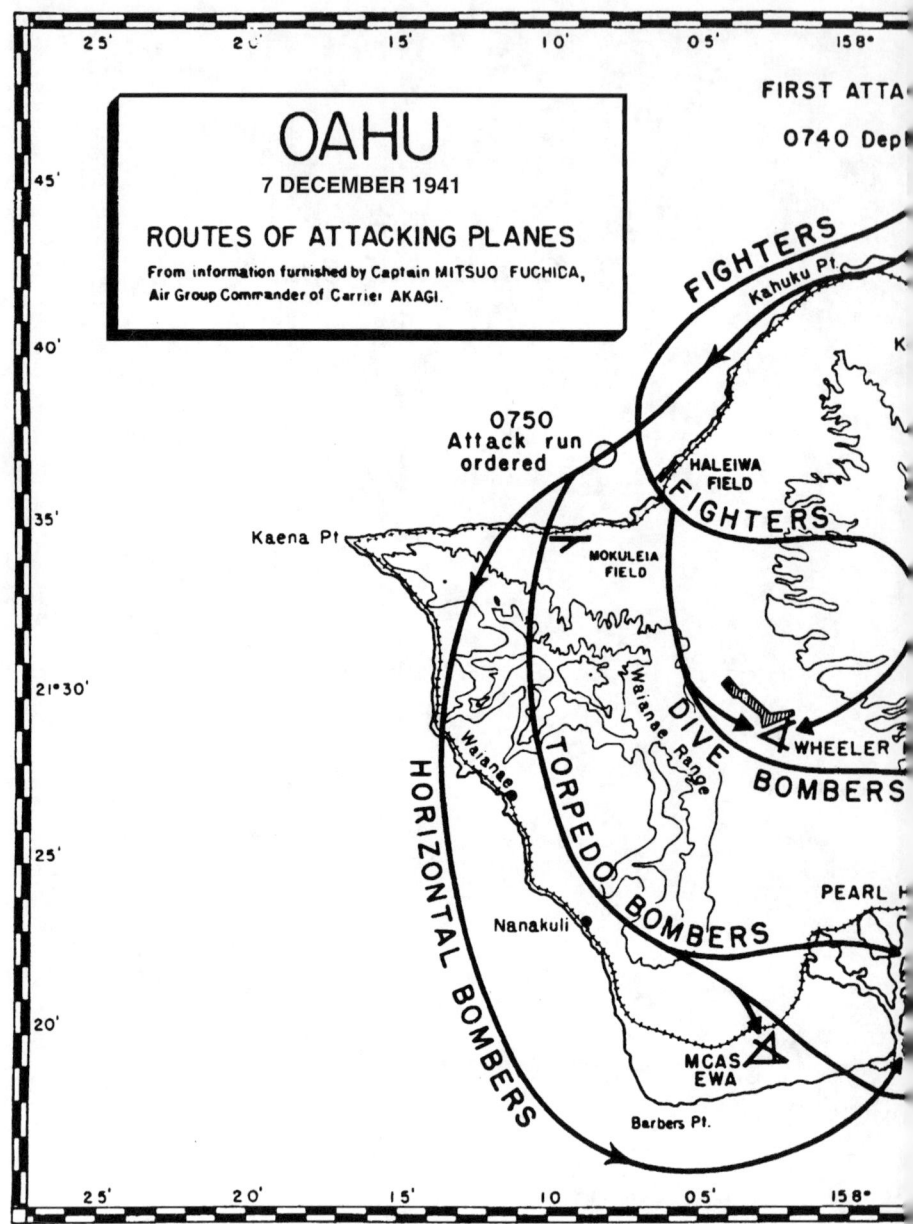

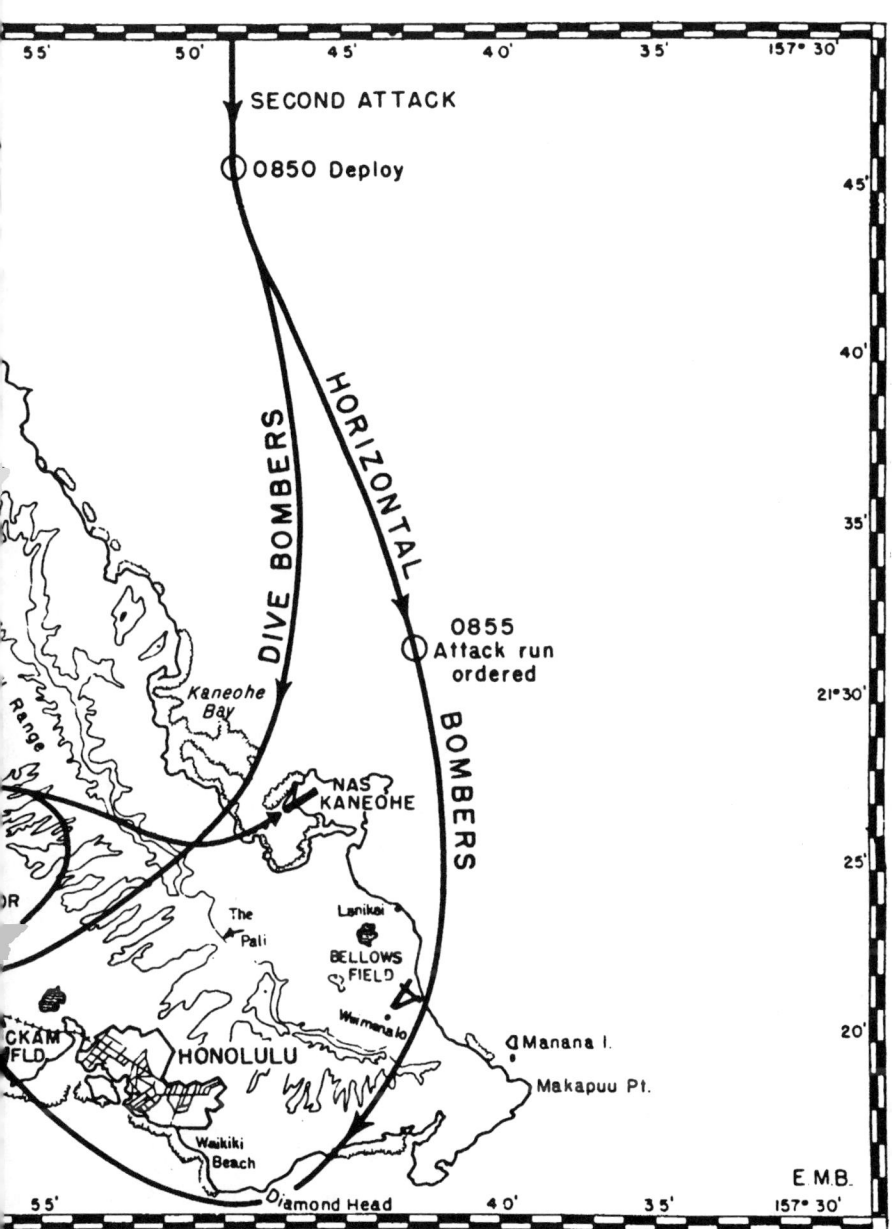

CONTENTS

PRELUDE TO WAR – POLITICAL MOVEMENTS   1

PRELUDE TO WAR – MILITARY MATTERS   19

INTELLIGENCE   36

AS ZERO HOUR APPROACHES   45

ATTACK ON PEARL HARBOR   51

AFTERWARDS   86

QUOTES   105

APPENDIXES
U.S. SHIPS IN PEARL HARBOR ON DECEMBER 7   121
HAWAII OPERATION TASK FORCE   122
MEDAL OF HONOR RECIPIENTS   123

BIBLIOGRAPHY   124

INDEX   126

PRELUDE TO WAR – POLITICAL MOVEMENTS

Q: What was "Hakko Ichiu"?
A: "Hakko Ichiu" or "Eight corners of the world under one roof" originated from Emperor Jimmu in about 600 B.C. and supported Japan's feeling that the Western Pacific should be controlled by the Asian countries in the area.

Q: What was one of the first recorded attempted invasions of Japan?
A: In 1281, the Mongolian Kublai Khan set sail from Korea with a great armada, intent on conquering Japan. A typhoon stopped the attempt. This "kamikaze" or "divine wind" was considered a good omen and reinforced Japan's idea that it was impregnable.

Q: What was the "Day of the Black Ships"?
A: In early 1853, Commodore Matthew G. Perry, with a flotilla of four black-painted ships, sailed into Tokyo Bay bearing a note from President Millard Fillmore requesting trade and consular facilities. Perry's arrival marked the end of centuries of feudal hermitage for Japan. Although Perry's visit is referred to as the "opening" of Japan, the first western visitor to Japan arrived in 1543 when a China-bound Portuguese ship was driven ashore by a storm.

Q: What was Japan's first international adventure?
A: Japan's brief war with China in 1894. Japan invaded China and occupied the Liaotung Peninsula and Port Arthur in Southern Manchuria. China could not resist Japan and gave up Southern Manchuria, Formosa and Korea. Germany, France and Russia did not want Japan to occupy Manchuria. The three countries' demands became known as "Triple Intervention." Japan gave back Manchuria but held on to Formosa and Korea.

Q: What was the "Open Door Policy"?
A: Britain, Germany, Russia, France, Italy, Japan and the United States agreed in 1900 that there would be no interference with normal commercial activity. This included giving all nations equal trade and development rights in China. Japan took particular offense as it felt it had special interests in China.

Q: Who labeled the Japanese the "Yellow Peril"?
A: The German Kaiser Wilhelm II coined this phrase on February 8, 1904, two days after Japan executed a sneak attack at Port Arthur. He was afraid that Japan's victory over Russia (which occurred in 1905) would upset western plans for exploitation of Asia. Both European and American press picked it up and used it in their media.

Q: What launched Japan into a major power?
A: A series of military victories including the Sino-Japanese War, the Russo-Japanese War, the annexation of Korea in 1910 and the annexation of German territories in the Pacific and China during World War I. Japan's victory over Russia made Japan a rival with the United States and Britain for control in the Pacific.

Q: What action established the United States as a Pacific power?
A: The annexation of Hawaii and the Philippines at the end of the 19th century.

Q: When did the United States begin to consider Japan a potential threat?
A: After Japan's gains in the Russo-Japanese War in 1905.

Q: Since the early 1900's, Hawaii was considered the most strategic location in the Pacific. What was its nickname?
A: The Gibraltar of the Pacific.

Q: What made the western powers consider Japan greedy?
A: Japan joined the Allies in August 1914, with little commitment to World War I. Japan's role was almost entirely naval: help patrol the Indian Ocean; "protect" Hong Kong and Shanghai; and occupy German claimed islands of Palau, Carolinas and the Marianas, including Truk and Saipan. Japan used this as an opportunity to seize Germany's Pacific possessions and the Shantung Province on mainland China.

Q: What was the Quota Act of 1924?
A: It prohibited further Japanese immigration into the United States. Japan took great insult to the Act's passage. Chinese had been excluded by the

Chinese Exclusion Act of 1882.

Q: In 1928, what pledge did Japan make?
A: To comply with the Kellogg-Briand Non-Aggression Pact. Japan was one of 15 nations which agreed to forego war and settle disputes by peaceful means.

Q: From the end of World War I until the 1930's, what prompted major shifts in Japanese opinion about the United States?
A: Americans didn't fully appreciate the humiliation that Japan suffered from the criticism on its role in China and the damage done by the western tariffs. The naval restrictions put on Japan from the London Naval Conference added to Japan's dissatisfaction.

Q: What was the purpose of the Washington Naval Conference of 1921-22 and the London Naval Conference of 1930?
A: The Washington Naval Conference was called by President Warren Harding to discuss a reduction of naval armaments and Pacific issues. Nine nations attended. Five nations (the United States, Britain, Japan, France and Italy) signed an agreement to observe a ten-year "naval holiday" in the construction of capital ships (those over 10,000 tons) and to fix a ratio of tonnage. Some of the signers had to scrap existing ships or ships under construction to meet the agreement. Four of the nations (the United States, Britain, France and Japan) agreed to respect each other's possessions in the Pacific and to confer should any conflicts arise. All nine participants, including Portugal, China, Belguim and the Netherlands, agreed to guarantee China's political independence and territorial rights, and agreed to follow the Open Door Policy. President Calvin Coolidge called another naval conference in Geneva in 1927 to discuss limiting the number of cruisers, destroyers and submarines. France and Italy declined to participate. During that conference, the United States, Britain and Japan could not agree to terms. The 1930 London Naval conference with Britain, the United States and Japan, again discussed fixing a ratio of ships among countries. Japan was not happy with the results.

Q: What was the Hawley-Smoot Tariff of 1930?
A: Enacted during the U.S. Great Depression, it was the highest tariff in United States history. The tariff had a serious impact on Japan which lacked many natural resources. Without an export trade, Japan could not buy the industrial material it needed. This encouraged Japanese expansionists.

Q: What was the League of Nations?
A: It was a part of the Treaty of Versailles. The conference at Versailles opened on January 18, 1919. Although 32 governments were represented, the conference was dominated by the United States, Britain, Italy and France. Japan, which had aligned its self with the Allies, was also present. The Versailles conference was intended to get reparations from Germany and its allies, divide up the territory of the conquered, and establish a League of Nations. The "heart of the Covenant of the League of Nations" required members to respect the territory of member nations. Although President Wilson was a strong mover in the development of the Covenant of the

League of Nations, which was signed on June 28, 1919, the United States Congress did not approve United States membership.

Q: Why did Japan withdraw from the League of Nations?
A: The League of Nations adopted the Lytton Report in February 1933, which criticized Japan for its military aggressiveness in China. Japan withdrew the next month in protest, feeling that expansion was necessary for survival.

Q: What confirmed the Western belief that Japan was aggressive and insincere in the 1930's?
A: The bombing of the Southern Manchurian railway at Mukden in 1931 and Japan's withdrawal from the League of Nations.

Q: What was the Stimson Doctrine?
A: Also referred to as the Non-Recognition Doctrine of 1932, it denounced Japan's actions in Manchuria. Henry Stimson, who was Secretary of State in 1932, hoped it would stir public opinion against Japan. Instead, it was viewed as a weak protest and it had no effect on Japan.

Q: What gave Japan the impression that America didn't have the guts to fight?
A: With the Japanese army's rapid conquest of Manchuria and then North China, Japan was bent on gaining as much territory as it could. Yet, even in 1932, when Japan and China were involved in heavy fighting, America did nothing except send its fleet to Shanghai.

Q: What excuse did Japan give for its invasion of Manchuria?
    a. National security
    b. Economic recession
    c. Need for more territory
A: Japan was in a hard economic recession in the 1930's. It deepened when the United States reduced American exports.

Q: What was the Trade Agreements Act of 1934?
A: Secretary of State Hull feared a tariff war. He encouraged, and Congress passed, the Trade Agreements Act which established reciprical trade agreements between the United States and those countries with which the United States traded most frequently. The Act also authorized the President to revise the tariffs without congressional approval.

Q: The United States Congress passed three Neutrality Acts, one in 1935, one in 1936 and one in 1937. Why were they enacted?
A: The acts reflected the American people's questions about why the United States got involved in World War I and indicated growing American support of an isolationist policy.

Q: What united the Chinese leaders Chiang Kai-shek and Mao Tse-Tung?
A: The two rivals met in Nanking in late September 1937 and agreed that their armies should join to fight the Japanese.

Q: What was the first indication that the United States was moving away from a neutral position in foreign policy?
A: President Roosevelt's famous "quarantine" speech which he delivered in Chicago on October 5, 1937. In it, Roosevelt suggested that the United States should use economic boycotts to solve international strife.

Q: On December 12, 1937, the Japanese deliberately bombed the USS *Panay* while it was patrolling the Yangtze River, killing three people aboard. What did the Americans do?
A: Instead of using the incident to start an international conflict with Japan, President Franklin D. Roosevelt accepted Japan's apology. Japan later paid the United States over two million dollars as compensation for the ship.

Q: What was the basic issue that separated Japan and the United States?
   a. Japan's alliance with Germany and Italy
   b. Equal commercial opportunity
   c. Japan's troops in China
A: The real problem was Japanese troops in China and Indochina.

Q: What was the "moral embargo"?
A: It was an embargo on the sale of airplanes and parts to any nation bombing civilians. Enacted on January 14, 1939, it was quickly followed by a stop of credit to Japan on February 7, 1939. On July 26, 1939, President Roosevelt announced that the Treaty of Commerce between Japan and the United States would be void after January 26, 1940.

Q: Why did the United States begin its embargoes?
A: Many Americans were upset that United States scrap iron, machine tools and petroleum products exported to Japan helped Japan's military build-up. Although those products were no longer exported to Japan after it joined Germany, oil was still exported. Japan continued to stock-pile oil and continued its military movements against Southern Indochina. On July 25, 1940, all Japanese assets in the United States were frozen, thus preventing Japan from purchasing United States oil and other goods.

Q: What were two major misconceptions held by the United States government?
A: 1) Japan would not dare attack the United States 2) Japan's involvement in China would keep it busy and stop further movements to the south.

Q: How did Germany affect Pearl Harbor?
A: Germany wanted Japan to attack the USSR in Siberia, but Germany had not defeated England and Japan didn't want to take the risk. Germany was also pressuring Japan to be more threatening toward the United States.

Q: Why did Japan sign an alliance with Germany in 1940?
A: In the hope that it would unify the country and make clear Japan's future course of action.

Q: What were the Anti-Comintern and the Tripartite Pacts?
A: The Anti-Comintern Pact was an agreement between Germany and Japan

to come to each other's aid in case of attack. The Tripartite Pact, signed September 27, 1940, was a similar treaty between Germany, Japan and Italy. They agreed to assist one another with all political, economic and military means if a power not then involved in the European or Sino-Japanese War attacked one of the treaty participants. The only major power not involved at that time was the United States.

Q: Why did Japan agree to the Tripartite Pact which obviously pointed to the United States?
A: To deter England and the United States from expanding in the Pacific. Foreign Minister Yosuke Matsuoka hoped the Soviet Union would also join and create a balance between the American and Eurasian continents. The closest he got was Japan's neutrality pact with the USSR. Instead, Japan became America's enemy, which encouraged China to hang on. When Germany attacked Russia, the USSR joined the Allies.

Q: What was the United States reaction to the Tripartite Pact?
A: The United States thought Japan's alliance with Nazi Germany and Fascist Italy meant Japan was interested in becoming a world power with these nations.

FACT: In July 1940, the U.S. Congress adopted the National Defense Act. It authorized the President to prohibit or limit the export of any material considered essential for national defense.

Q: What two Acts, passed by the United States Congress in 1940, proved most helpful in preparing the United States for war?
A: The first was the Selective Training and Service Act (commonly called the draft), which required all men between the ages of 21 to 35 to register for military service. The second was the Armaments Appropriations Act, which set aside 1.8 billion dollars for the construction of ships and the purchase of weapons.

Q: Who controlled Japanese national policy and why?
A: The Meiji Constitution dictated: 1) the Army and Navy Ministers must be active duty officers, and 2) the cabinet could not convene without those ministers. To balance the power, only the Emperor, as Supreme Commander, could declare war.

Q: Who was responsible for the Emperor's naval operations?
A: The Chief of the Naval General Staff. After the China Incident in 1937, the Imperial General Headquarters was established with membership composed of the Chiefs of the Army and Navy General Staffs and the Ministers of War and Navy. Because of the structure, the Chief of the Naval General Staff ended up presenting the plan to attack Hawaii to the Chief of the Army General Staff and to the Ministers of War and Navy.

Admiral Osami Nagano, Chief, Navy General Staff.
National Archives

Q: What is "Showa" or "enlightened peace"?
A: "Showa", which translates to "enlightened peace", was Emperor Hirohito's word to characterize his reign.

Q: What were the Zaibatsu?
A: Twelve families in Japan who controlled big business. Their families shaped Japan's economy into a ready instrument for war. The Zaihatsu's profit came from the direct supply of ship equipment and materials to embattled nations of Europe and through expansion into those nations' traditional markets in Asia.

Q: Who were the three crows and how did they influence Japanese policy?
A: Three gentlemen named Nagata, Obata and Okamura. They were Japanese attaches in Europe who were responsible for modernizing the armed forces. General Hideki Tojo's rise to leadership of the Army as Chief of the Army Staff and Minister of War was due to their influence on Emperor Hirohito. Tojo was also supported by the Zaibatsu.

Q: What did many consider the biggest error of the advisers to Emperor Hirohito?
A: That General Tojo was chosen, on October 14, 1941, to run the government as Prime Minister while keeping his position as Minister of War.

General Hideki Tojo, Minister of War 1941.
National Archives

Q: **In 1941, why didn't the United States take Japan's military build-up more seriously?**

A: When Japan announced its national policy to secure an "Empire of the East Asia Continent by diplomatic policy, national defense, mutually dependent on each other as well as advance and develop the Empire toward the South Sea" on August 11, 1936, no one got excited. The world was used to seeing Japan's build-up. It had shown aggressive military behavior in Asia from 1931.

FACT: Vice Admiral Shigetaro Shimada, the Navy Minister when Japan went to war, thought Japan should declare war on Britain and the Netherlands, but not the United States. If the United States struck first, Japan could declare war with honor. Even if the United States could be kept out of the war initially, it was certain that it could not remain a spectator and would inevitably join the Allies. Japan's only hope for victory was to delay America's entry as long as possible.

Vice Admiral Shigetaro Shimada, Navy Minister
at the time of the attack. National Archives

Q: What prompted Japan's aggressive behavior and expansion into China, Southeast Asia, Malaya, the Philippines and the Dutch East Indies?
A: The economic barriers established by other countries because of the world economic crisis in the early 1930's kept Japan from getting raw materials it needed. Japan attacked China since China supplied most of Japan's cotton and also had coal and iron. Japan wanted Indochina for its rice, tin, rubber and sugar. Japan felt that, for its own survival, it had to acquire the oil and other natural resources of Southeast Asia, Malaya, the Philippines and the Dutch East Indies. This was the only way Japan could face its rivals, the United States, England and the Soviet Union.

Q: What actions did the United States take as Japan continued its expansionist policy?
A: When Henry Stimson was appointed Secretary of War in 1940, he encouraged President Roosevelt toward war with Japan. On July 23, 1941, the Japanese forced the Vichy Government to allow Japanese troops peaceful entry into French-occupied Indochina. Roosevelt had to do something. He ordered all Japanese assets in America frozen on July 26, 1941, cutting off Japan's main supply of oil and he closed the Panama Canal to Japanese shipping.

Henry Stimson, Secretary of War.
National Archives

FACT: Although Japan's involvement in Indochina indicated its expansionist ambitions in Asia, some Japanese cabinet members were willing to change Japan's agressive military policies. However, General Tojo, as Prime Minister, was in charge and he was not going to allow the cabinet to alter the course set.

Q: What was the "Essentials of the Policy toward the South Seas"?
A: It was Japan's South Seas policy for a rapid expansion of the empire's overall defense capacity. It did not include use of arms unless Japan was threatened by embargoes or by Allied Forces.

Q: What was the curse of Japan's foreign policy?
A: Japan's invasion of China. Japan would not try to settle the war by negotiat-

ing with Chiang Kai-shek. Instead Japan felt that if the Americans would discontinue aid to the Chinese nationalist government, China would be forced to come to an agreement with Japan.

Q: What did Secretary of State Hull think would be the outcome of Japan's invasion of China?
A: He thought Japan would eventually win. He also knew that the United States was not interested enough in China to intervene.

Q: What might have happened if the United States had limited its exports during Japan's build-up?
A: Even if the United States had only limited its exports to Japan to normal peace-time limits, Japan would never have been able to stock pile enough material to support its campaigns in China while building up the Japanese navy.

Q: Why did Secretary Hull encourage actions which would keep Japan in China?
A: By keeping Japan busy in China, Hull thought Japan would not continue its Southeast Asia expansion. He was afraid that Germany might take over the Suez Canal, giving Germany access to the raw materials in the Pacific and, at the same time, cutting Britain off from those resources.

FACT: The relationship between Japan and the United States was aggravated by United States financial aid to China and by United States volunteers fighting with the Chinese. The United States also continued to purchase Southeast Asian resources while continuing economic sanctions against Japan.

Q: What year was 1941 in the Japanese calendar?
A: It was the 2,601st anniversary of the founding of the Japanese Empire.

Q: In the Buddhist calendar, what year is 1941?
        a. The year of the Snake
        b. The year of the Dragon
        c. The year of the Monkey
A: The year of the Snake.

Q: Why did Japan's militarists want to go to war quickly?
A: So that the United States, Britain and the Netherlands could not have time to grow stronger.

Q: Who was Stanley D. Hornbeck?
A: Hornbeck was chief of the State Departments Far East Division and Secretary of State Hull's chief advisor. He believed that a strong military was necessary to affect Japan's policy toward China. Hornbeck's only experience with China was as a teacher. Hornbeck advised Hull that the United States should keep Japan occupied by aiding China. That way, Japan would be less likely to go to war with the United States or Britain.

Q: What advantage did Ambassador Grew have when he was assigned to be the United States Ambassador to Japan?
A: His wife, Alice, was the granddaughter of Commodore Perry and she spoke fluent Japanese. Grew was ambassador from 1932 - 1941.

Ambassador Joseph C. Grew.
National Archives

Q: Through whom did Ambassador Grew learn that there was a possible attack on Pearl Harbor?
    a. President Roosevelt
    b. Secretary Stimson
    c. Richardo Rivera-Schreiber
A: The Honorable Richardo Rivera-Schreiber, Peru's Minister to Japan. On January 27, 1941, Schreiber advised Max Bishop, third secretary of the American Embassy, that his intelligence sources had just learned that the Japanese had a war plan involving a surprise attack on Pearl Harbor.

Q: In early 1941, why did Japan sign a Treaty of Neutrality with Stalin's government?
A: To ensure against Russian intervention in the Greater East Asia design.

FACT: Secretary of State Hull hoped for years that the Japanese would get so tired of the war with China that they would overthrow their leaders. Because of Hull's inflexibility, and encouraged by his chief advisor, Hornbeck, he could not consider the possibility of working out a peaceful coexistence with Japan.

Q: When Ambassador Grew wrote to Washington on January 27, 1941 to warn of the possible attack, less than three weeks had passed after Admiral Yamamoto wrote to Admiral Ogawa, Navy Minister, about his plans to attack Pearl Harbor. Why was Grew's warnings not taken seriously?
A: No one believed that the Minister from Peru, who had passed the information, could find out such information, especially since it was attributed to a conversation overheard by a Japanese cook.

Q: Who was Japan's ambassador to the United States on December 7, 1941?
    a. Fumimaro Konoye
    b. Kichisaburo Nomura
    c. Saburo Kurusu

A: Ambassador Kichisaburo Nomura. He was appointed Ambassador to the United States in November 1940. Admiral Nomura (RET) had told Foreign Minister Yosuke Matsuoka for months that he didn't want the job. Nomura had lived in the United States and had many American friends, including President Roosevelt. He was a sincere man, well liked, respected and a peace advocate. He was sent to Washington to discuss ways to avoid war in the Pacific. When he left Japan he was not very optimistic. Kurusu was a special envoy. Konoye was the Prime Minister before General Tojo.

Q: Why was special envoy Kurusu sent to the United States?
A: At Ambassador Nomura's request, Kurusu was sent to assist Nomura because Nomura was a respected military officer but he was not a professional diplomat. Kurusu was. Ironically, Kurusu also had American ties. His wife was an American, a native of Chicago.

Q: When did Honolulu's new Consul General from Japan arrive?
A: Nagao Kita disembarked from *Tatuta Maru,* Japan's most ultra-modern passenger ship, on March 14, 1941.

Q: In April 1941, the first official proposal was made by the United States to Japan. Developed by Secretary of State Hull, what were the four principles for negotiations?
A: (1) Respect for the territorial integrity and the sovereignty of each and all nations;
(2) Support of the principles of non-interference in the internal affairs of other countries;
(3) Support of the principle of equality including equality of commercial opportunity;
(4) Non-disturbance of the status quo in the Pacific except as the status quo may be altered by peaceful means.

FACT: Foreign Minister Yosuke Matsuoka had directed Ambassador Nomura to seek a peaceful solution with the United States. When he learned of Secretary Hull's June 21, 1941 terms, in which Hull expressed United States concern about certain Japanese cabinet members who were committed to Germany, he was deeply offended. On July 12, 1941, Matsuoka shocked the Japanese Liaison Conference by suggesting that Japan immediately break off negotiations with the United States. Matsuoka was replaced by Vice Admiral Teijiro Toyoda, and negotiations continued.

Q: In early September 1941, Admiral Yamamoto had a secret meeting with Prince Konoye. What was discussed?
A: Although a member of the royal family, Prince Konoye took the position of Prime Minister in June 1937. He resigned in January 1939, then returned to office of Prime Minister in July 18, 1940. Yamamoto discussed a possible meeting between Konoye and President Roosevelt.

Q: What was the "Outline of the Imperial Policy to Meet with the New (World) Situation"?
A: Developed on July 2, 1941 between the Imperial Headquarters and the civilian government, Japan proposed to prepare for war with the United States

while maintaining the southward expansion policy.

Q: How and when was the attack on Pearl Harbor briefed by Prime Minister/Minister of War Tojo to Emperor Hirohito?
A: Prime Minister Tojo and his Cabinet had a month to develop Japan's war plans. At the end of August the plans were presented to the Emperor. Pearl Harbor was simply listed as one target among a seemingly endless list of targets, even though plans for the Pearl Harbor attack were well under way.

Q: What was Britain prepared to do if the United States declared war against Japan and left England to fight Germany alone?
A: The British were planning to leak the details of Rainbow 5 to the Germans, showing an American/British plot that the United States was preparing to enter the war against Germany.

Q: Who participated in the ABC - 1 staff talks?
    a. America, Britain, Canada
    b. America, Britain, China
    c. All the British Commonwealth
A: America, Britain and Canada. The meetings discussed America's commitment to the defense of Anglo/American interests in the Far East, including Singapore and the Philippines. The results of those staff talks formed the basis for Rainbow 5.

Q: What was the Japanese "Outline of the Execution Plan of the Imperial Policy"?
A: Proposed on September 6, 1941, it directed that all preparations for war against the United States be completed by October 1941, and that if war against the United States seemed inevitable by early November, it be initiated immediately. The "Outline" plan was adopted on November 5, 1941. It also specified that negotiations with the United States must be completed by December 1.

Q: America thought that Prime Minister Konoye's anxiety to get a quick settlement meant that time was on the American's side. Konoye wanted a peaceful solution. What happened to him?
A: On October 12, 1941, Prime Minister Konoye invited his ministers to his home in hopes of resolving the conflicts among them. It wasn't successful and on October 23, 1941, Konoye was replaced by militant General Hideki Tojo. Tojo ran his cabinet like a dictatorship and forced all the liberals out.

Q: How did Japan hope to prevent international censure for the surprise attack?
A: International law experts maintained that it was legal to declare war if the declaration preceded the commencement of hostilities — even if only one or one-half second in advance; the time interval was not important. Since the Hawaii Operation obviously could not be conducted without surprise, Japan had to open hostilities with the Pearl Harbor attack. Japan believed that the operation could be carried out within international law if the declaration could be sent to the United States at the last moment, thus preventing the United States from having enough time to prepare countermeasures.

Q: How did China affect President Roosevelt's relationship with Japan?
A: Chiang Kai-shek had many supporters in the United States. China's ambassador in Washington, Hu Shih, promoted the Open Door Policy and advocated peaceful change. He also wanted Japan out of China. Roosevelt's final proposal to Japan demanded Japan's withdrawal from China and the sole recognition of Chiang Kai-shek's government.

Q: How did China mislead the United States about Japan's fighting capability?
A: Chiang Kai-shek's government was intent on keeping United States support and misled the United States by telling it that Japan was using much of its resources in China. Actually, only a small portion of Japan's troops had been committed to China.

Q: England's Winston Churchill's November 25 telegram to Roosevelt emphasized the China issue. Why, when China was a non-negotiable item for Japan and his action was sure to provoke war?
A: Churchill wanted to ensure continued good will with the United States since it was necessary for the survival of England. He was supporting the past position of the United States.

FACT: At a November 25, 1941 conference, President Roosevelt and his "war cabinet" discussed how the United States should maneuver Japan into "firing the first shot" without too much danger to Americans. Roosevelt's advisors felt it was important for the American public to know who was the aggressor.

Q: What unusual request was made of the United States Census Bureau?
A: On November 26, 1941, the Census Bureau was told that, by order of President Roosevelt, it was to compile a list of all Japanese in the United States, by state. The list was compiled for possible future internment of Japanese in concentration camps.

Q: In 1941, Japan submitted to the United States "Proposal B". What was it?
A: Japan agreed to withdraw their troops from the southern half of Indochina if the United States would unfreeze Japanese assets, allow American oil shipments, help Japan procure materials and oil from the Dutch East Indies, and stop sending aid to China.

FACT: On November 20, 1941, the Japanese envoys in Washington presented Proposal B to Secretary Hull. In an effort to buy more time for the United States military build-up in the Philippines, Hull developed a modus vivendi for President Roosevelt's approval, as a temporary means of getting along with Japan. This proposal never made it beyond the planning stages. On November 26, 1941, Roosevelt learned that Japan had sent 30-50 ships to Formosa. Angered with Japan's actions, he abandoned the idea and refused to discuss Japan's Proposal B.

Q: What was the "Hull Note"?
A: The "Hull Note" was President Roosevelt's answer to Japan's Proposal B. Developed by Secretary Hull and his advisors, it was delivered to Ambassador Nomura on November 26. The Ten Point document demanded an

immediate and unconditional withdrawal from Indochina and all China before sanctions would be lifted. The Japanese interpreted this to mean the United States required them to retreat to where they stood in January 1931.

Secretary of State Cordell Hull with Ambassador Kichisaburo Nomura to the left and Special Envoy Saburo Kurusu to the right.

Q: **To whom was the "Hull Note" directed?**
A: Foreign Minister Shigenori Togo. Ironically, Togo had been called back from Germany in 1930 for being anti-Nazi. He was also recalled from Russia in 1940 with other ambassadors who were considered "too friendly" to Britain and the United States.

FACT: When Secretary Hull's "Hull Note" was forwarded to Prime Minister Tojo, it was rejected. Foreign Minister Togo alerted Ambassador Nomura that a fourteen part message would be forthcoming. Through an intelligence intercept, President Roosevelt received thirteen of the fourteen parts on December 6, 1941. His reaction, "This means war..."

Cordell Hull, Secretary of State.
National Archives

Q: How many Japanese-Americans were in Hawaii on December 7?
    a. Approximately 160,000
    b. Approximately 225,000
    c. Over 500,000
A: Approximately 160,000 Japanese, or about forty per cent of the population living in the Territory of Hawaii on December 7, 1941. Thirty-seven thousand five hundred were foreign born.

Q: On the eve of Pearl Harbor, what looked like the only two alternatives for preventing war?
A: The United States could ignore Japan's violation of the Nonaggression Pact of 1928 or Japan had to abandon China.

Q: When did President Roosevelt decide that future talks between Japan and the United States would be fruitless?
A: The President knew on November 27. American Intelligence had eavesdropped on a telephone conversation between the Japanese Foreign Office and Ambassador Nomura's assistant, Kurusu.

Q: What was President Roosevelt's main preoccupation in the week beginning December 1?
A: Realizing war was imminent, Roosevelt was planning for Japanese military aggression.

Q: On December 5, 1941, President Roosevelt sent a message to Emperor Hirohito, through Ambassador Grew, in a last-minute effort to avoid conflict. What happened to the message?
A: The Japanese Post Office normally handled telegrams one hour after receiving them. Roosevelt's message was marked "triple priority." The Japanese telegraph office stamped it received at 1200 on December 6. Ambassador Grew did not receive it until 2230.

Q: Why was President Roosevelt's message delayed?
A: On November 29, the chief of the Ministry of Communications Censorship Office was directed to delay the delivery of all incoming and outgoing cables by five hours, except Japanese government messages. The schedule was changed again on December 6. On one day, there would be a five-hour delay and, on the next day, a ten-hour delay. This made December 6, in Japan, the day for a ten-hour delay. Roosevelt's message left the Post Office for delivery to Ambassador Grew at 2100.

Q: How was Ambassador Grew notified that President Roosevelt was sending a message to Emperor Hirohito?
A: On December 7, (December 6, in Hawaii) at about 1500, Grew was listening to San Francisco radio station KGEI, when he heard a report that the president had sent a message to the Emperor and that Grew was to deliver it.

Q: Once Ambassador Grew received the telegram, he immediately met with Foreign Minister Shigenori Togo. What was his request?
A: An audience with Emperor Hirohito, which was his right as an ambassador. Togo grudgingly agreed to arrange the meeting.

Q: What was the "pilot" message?
A: This was Foreign Minister Togo's message alerting Ambassador Nomura to expect, on the following day, a fourteen-part message concerning the proposals Secretary of State Hull submitted to the Japanese Government on November 26.

Q: At what time was the last part of the fourteen-part message relaying Tokyo's reply to Washington's final proposal sent to Ambassador Nomura?
A: The United States Naval Station in Bainbridge Island, Washington, intercepted the message between 0304 and 0310 on the morning of December 7, and teletyped it in the Japanese code to the Navy de-cryptors in Washington, D.C. It was translated by 0730 Eastern Standard Time (EST). The Japanese Embassy in Washington, D.C. received their message between 0700 and 0800 EST.

Q: Once the leaders in Washington received all of the fourteen-part message, if they had picked up the phone and called, instead of sending cables, how much time would the military commanders in Hawaii have had to prepare for the attack?
A: At least an hour's preparation time, assuming that Hawaii would have taken it seriously and gone on full alert status at once.

Q: What exactly did the fourteenth-part say?
A: "The Japanese Government regrets to have to notify hereby the American Government that in view of the attitude of the American Government it cannot but consider that it is impossible to reach an agreement through further negotiations."

Q: At what time did the army command in Washington, D.C. receive the fourteenth-part?
A: At approximately 0830 EST, on December 7.

Q: What was the reaction of many of the high-ranking officials in Washington, when they were given the fourteenth part?
A: Most felt that the message was relatively unimportant.

Q: Why didn't anyone call Hawaii to see if Hawaii was on alert?
A: Everyone assumed Hawaii was on alert.

Q: How long was General George C. Marshall, the Army's Chief of Staff, told it would take to deliver a message to Hawaii warning of the termination of political relationships with Japan?
        a. Between ten to fifteen minutes
        b. Between thirty and forty minutes
        c. Over an hour
A: Marshall was told that by using normal procedures it would take between 30 to 40 minutes.

Q: Why didn't General Marshall telephone his warning instead of relying on cables?
A: Marshall didn't trust telephones and hated using them. He had more faith in the speed of the Army Signal Corps.

FACT: At 0800 December 7, Ambassador Nomura received the fourteenth-part of the lengthy message. Although Japan intended to have the message delivered to the United States government by 1300 December 7, the delivery was delayed because it took a long time to get it typed. Only a few Japanese personnel had the security authorization to type it. In addition, the embassy personnel had had a big party the night before and were suffering the after-effects.

Q: What caused the delay in sending the "war warning" message to Oahu?
A: The army found that atmospheric conditions had cut off the message channel to Honolulu from around 1030 that morning. The officer in charge of the War Department Signal Center decided to send the message through commercial service for quicker transmission. The commercial service had a direct teletype to San Francisco and there the message could be turned over to RCA, which would send it to Honolulu.

Q: Roosevelt was President on December 7, 1941. Who was the Vice President?
A: Henry Wallace.

Q: Who was the Territorial Governor of Hawaii at the time of the attack?
    a. Joseph B. Poindexter
    b. William A. Gabrielson
    c. Lester Petrie
A: Poindexter was Governor. Petrie was the Mayor of Honolulu and Gabrielson was the Chief of Police.

PRELUDE TO WAR – MILITARY MATTERS

Q: Pearl Harbor is one of the few natural harbors in Hawaii. When did it become military property?
A: Through a 1887 Reciprocity Treaty between the United States and the Kingdom of Hawaii. The United States acquired exclusive rights to establish and maintain a coal and repair station in Pearl Harbor for United States vessels. The coaling station would be called the Pearl Harbor Naval Station rather than Puuloa, the original Hawaiian name for the harbor.

Q: Pearl Harbor was considered an excellent naval base. What was its one major drawback?
A: If a ship was sunk in its narrow entrance, it would "lock the door" on the harbor for weeks, if not months. No ships or boats could enter or leave.

Aerial view of Pearl Harbor taken two months before the attack.
National Archives

Q: As early as 1890, how did Admiral Alfred T. Mahan warn the United States about Japan's rise to power?
A: In his book The Influence of the Sea Power Upon History, Mahan predicted Japan's rise to power. He felt the United States had to have a strong naval force if it was to expand into the Pacific before Japan. Mahan stressed the United States should do three things: get the Panama Canal built so the United States Fleet could move quickly into the Pacific; take over the Philippines and Hawaii (which was then an independent nation); and take Cuba to defend the Canal.

Q: What was the "Port Arthur Incident"?
A: On February 8, 1904, while diplomats were still negotiating in Moscow, a Japanese battle fleet struck the Russian Pacific Squadron lying at anchor in Port Arthur. War was not formally declared by Japan until February 10, 1904. Port Arthur fell on December 31, 1904. Mukden, the capital of Manchuria, fell on March 16, 1905. Russia sent its fleet to join the fight. On May 27, 1905, Admiral Heihachiro Togo destroyed most of the Russian fleet in a two-day battle at Tsushima Straits. Japan lost over 200,000 men. President Theodore Roosevelt brought Russia and Japan together to negotiate a settlement. On September 5, 1905, the Russo-Japanese War was ended by the signing of the Treaty of Portsmouth.

Q: When was the last time the Japanese navy saw serious action before Pearl Harbor?
        a.   1905
        b.   1927
        c.   1939

A: In 1905, during the Russo-Japanese War.

Q: What was the United States opinion about the surprise attacks that the Japanese used in the Sino-Japanese War of 1894-95 and in the Russo-Japanese War of 1904-05?
A: Brilliant tactical maneuvers. American military in the 1920's and 1930's carried out maneuvers based on simulated Japanese attacks on Pearl Harbor that were surprisingly close to the real one.

Q: What was the first United States aircraft carrier?
A: The collier USS *Jupiter*, which was refitted and commissioned the aircraft carrier USS *Langley* in 1922.

Q: When was the USS Arizona built?
A: The 608 foot-long battleship was originally built in 1916 and modernized in 1931.

Q: The Pearl Harbor Submarine Base was built during 1920-1922, mainly from salvaged World War I materials. Whom did the Navy pick to run this monumental task?
A: A thirty-five year old Lieutenant Commander named Chester W. Nimitz.

Q: What was the 1931 Invasion of Manchuria?
A: On September 18, 1931, a Chinese unit patrolling the South Manchurian Railroad in Mukden, capital of Manchuria, heard a loud explosion. When they went to investigate, they found that railroad tracks had been dynamited. Japanese troops then began firing upon the Chinese.

Q: Why was the incident viewed with suspicion?
A: On the same day of the attack, the Japanese Consul General in Mukden told Tokyo that an incident might occur while Kwangtung Army units were carrying out maneuvers in the Mukden area. Within a few hours after the fighting broke out, Japanese forces overcame the Chinese in the Chinese barracks near where the explosion occurred. By the next day, the city and airfield were in Japanese hands. Manchuria was renamed Manchukuo and Japan declared it an independent state under Japanese protection.

Q: What lesson should have been learned from the Grand Joint Exercise Number Four?
A: The exercise was a large-scale exercise between the United States Army and Navy. It was conducted from February 1 to 12, 1932. The commander of the attack force was Admiral H. E. Yarnell. Rather than follow navy tradition, Yarnell selected an aircraft carrier for his headquarters, instead of a battleship. He headed out to Honolulu from California on the USS Saratoga, accompanied by the USS Lexington and an escort of destroyers, leaving behind his battleships and cruisers. On February 7, 1932 (a Sunday), a half-hour before dawn, Yarnell launched 152 planes into the dark. Although the defenders expected some sort of air attack, they were caught by surprise because the clouds over the mountain range covered the approaching planes. The planes "attacked" the Army airfields and the area near Pearl Harbor just as dawn was breaking. Most of the defenders' planes were on

the ground and unprepared. Japan's attack on Pearl Harbor, ten years later, was almost a perfect duplicate of Yarnell's strategy.

Q: What country did the Japanese Navy use as a model when it organized its military structure?
    a. America
    b. Britain
    c. Russia
A: The Japanese Imperial Navy patterned itself after the British Navy as the best model for the Japanese character and requirements. The Army was patterned after the Prussian Army.

Q: In 1935, a 50-year-old unhappy staff officer, suffering a mid-life crisis, was assigned as G-2, Director of Intelligence, for the Hawaiian Department. He drew up a plan to maintain internal security and censorship against subversion by the Japanese community, should the United States and Japan go to war. His plan included the arrest and internment of certain persons of the "orange race" (Japanese) who were dangerous to American interests and to retain them in custody as hostages, rather than POWs. Who was he?
A: The officer's name was Patton, later known world-wide as General George S. Patton, one of the leading generals of World War II.

Q: Were the first shots fired between Americans and Japanese on December 7, 1941?
A: No. On December 12, 1937, pre-dating Pearl Harbor by almost four years to the day, the USS Panay, a Yangtze River gunboat, was bombed and sunk near Hankow by Japanese military anxious to start a war.

Q: What was the "China Incident"?
A: On July 7, 1937, a Japanese detachment, carrying out night exercises near the Marco Polo Bridge southwest of Peking, was allegedly fired upon by Chinese troops. Some suspect the incident was manufactured by Japanese commanders in the area. Although the next day both Japanese and Chinese commanders resolved the matter, political leaders used the event to begin the "China Incident", or Japan's invasion of China.

Q: How did the philosophy of "Bushido" affect Japan's actions in preparing for war?
A: "Bushido", or "way of the warrior" symbolized Japan's feelings that it would win and rule its world according to the Samurai Code: ruthlessness, honor, self discipline, courage, sacrifice, physical endurance and ambition.

Q: To what country did "Minami" refer?
    a. Russia
    b. China
    c. United States of America
A: It was Japan's name for the United States

Q: What was the Hawaiian Detachment?
A: From October 1939, this unit consisted of a carrier, heavy cruisers and

destroyers. It was responsible for maintaining Pearl Harbor until the fleet arrived in 1940. Popularly called the "Pineapple Fleet", it was commanded by Vice Admiral Adolphus Andrews in 1940.

Q: Wheeler and Kaneohe were major secondary targets during the December 7 attack. When were they established?
A: Wheeler Airfield became a permanent military installation in 1939. It provided protection for Hickam and later Pearl Harbor, when the fleet shifted from the west coast to Hawaii in the summer of 1940. Kaneohe Naval Air Station was established in 1939 as a seaplane facility.

Q: When was Admiral Isoroku Yamamoto appointed Commander-in-Chief of the Combined Fleet?
    a.   In June 1932
    b.   In August 1939
    c.   In January 1941
A: In August 1939.

Q: What gave Admiral Yamamoto the idea that an attack on Pearl Harbor would work?
A: Britain's naval attack on the Italian fleet anchored in Taranto Harbor, Italy, on November 12, 1940. In less than an hour, 50 per cent of Italy's battleships were disabled for six months. This attack alerted American military leaders to the hazards of air attacks on ships.

Q: What was the Lang Son Incident?
A: General Akito Nakamura led his troops in an attack against French troops at Lang Son, in September 1940, just as the French Governor, General Decoux, was conceding to the "Matsuoka-Henry" agreement which was signed August 30, 1940 between France and Japan. The agreement permitted a small number of Japanese troops into Indochina.

Q: Why did the United States place so much concentration on the South China Sea area in the summer of 1941?
A: Because of the major Japanese troop movement in the French Indochina area.

Q: What was Japan's response when asked why it was deploying its troops?
A: Japan maintained that its interest was only in self-defense and merely to counter any threat by the Chinese.

FACT: By 1940, Admiral Yamamoto began to think of offensive strategies. He was influenced by Hector C. Bywater and Homer Lea. Hector Bywater published a book called *The Great Pacific War*. In it, Bywater discussed war strategies in the Pacific, and predicted Japan would make a surprise attack on Pearl Harbor, as well as Guam and the Philippines. Yamamoto studied the book and used many of Bywater's strategies. If Yamamoto had not been influenced by Bywater, he may have decided on an initial attack on the Dutch East Indies instead of Pearl Harbor. Had that happened, the United States' interest and participation in the conflict would have been very different. Homer Lea published a fictional history in 1909 describing Japanese plans to conquer the United States. The book, *Valor of Ignorance,* predicted that the Japanese could easily take the Philippines, Hawaii and Alaska and gain control of the northern Pacific. The Japanese also published Lea's book, calling it *The War Between Japan and America.* It caught the interest of military on both sides.

Admiral Isoroku Yamamoto, Commander-in-chief, Combined Fleet. National Archives

Q: **In 1941, how much of a reserve oil supply did the Japanese navy have?**
    a. 18 months
    b. 30 months
    c. 5 years
A: Eighteen months supply. Much of Japan's actions during this period can be related to its desperate need for oil.

Q: **Who commanded the Fleet in 1940?**
    a. Admiral James O. Richardson
    b. Admiral Husband Kimmel
    c. Admiral Harold R. Stark
A: Admiral Richardson took command of the United States Fleet on January 6, 1940.

Q: **Why was Admiral Richardson more comfortable keeping the fleet in Lahaina rather than Pearl Harbor?**
A: Because it was easier for the fleet to reach open waters in case of emergency.

Q: **Why was Admiral Richardson relieved of command early?**
A: Richardson misjudged how much personal criticism President Roosevelt would take. He disagreed with the President about the readiness of the navy to defend itself and advocated that the principal ships of the Fleet could do a better job of preparing for war by returning to their west coast bases than by being kept out in Hawaiian waters.

Q: **What was "Plan Dog"?**
A: A plan developed by Admiral Harold Stark, Chief of Naval Operations, on actions the United States should take to support the Allies and to prepare for the likely event of the United States joining World War II. Stark proposed that the United States should plan on sending light naval forces and

aircraft to Great Britain. He felt a final victory for the Allies depended on Britain's survival.

Q: **What was Rear Admiral Kimmel doing when informed that he was to be the Commander-in-Chief of the United States Fleet (CINCUS)?**
A: Kimmel was Commander of Cruisers, Battle Force. He was playing golf with his Chief of Staff, Captain Walter Delany, when he was notified of his selection. Kimmel was hand-picked by President Roosevelt, who had known him when Roosevelt was an Assistant Secretary of the Navy. Kimmel was selected over 32 more senior admirals.

Q: **As CINCUS, what was Admiral Kimmel's assessment of his air reconnaissance capability?**
A: Shortly after Admiral Kimmel took command on February 1, 1941, he realized he was losing reconnaissance aircraft necessary for early warning, and he was concerned that attack forces might be gathering in the Pacific. He had 36 planes and the Hawaiian Air Force had an additional 21 commissioned B-18s. That same month, Admiral Stark told Kimmel that the Japanese did not plan an attack in the foreseeable future. On December 7, the only aerial reconnaissance was a short flight south of Pearl Harbor, a flight 180-degrees in the wrong direction.

Q: **What was Admiral Kimmel called by his friends?**
A: He attended Annapolis, graduating thirteenth out of the sixty-two graduates of the class of 1904. His midshipman's nickname was Hubby. To most of his friends, he was known as Kim. Kimmel was a brilliant strategist and a fighter. This later affected the outcome of Pearl Harbor because he always envisioned attacking from Pearl Harbor, and it is doubtful it ever occurred to him that he would be put in a defensive position.

Admiral Husband E. Kimmel, Command-in-Chief, United States Fleet (CINCUS). National Archives

Q: **Who had been an Annapolis classmate of Admiral Kimmel?**
    a. President Franklin Roosevelt
    b. Admiral Chester Nimitz
    c. Vice Admiral William Halsey

A: Admiral Kimmel tried to go to West Point. When that fell through, he tried for the United States Naval Academy, and this time he succeeded. His classmate was William Halsey.

Q: **When did Lieutenant General Walter C. Short take command of the Hawaiian Department?**
    a. 1935
    b. 1939
    c. 1941

A: On February 7, 1941, one week after Admiral Kimmel took command of the fleet.

Lieutenant General Walter C. Short, Commanding General, Hawaiian Department. National Archives

Q: **Where was the home station of the United States Fleet in 1940?**
    a. San Pedro, California
    b. San Francisco, California
    c. Seattle, Washington

A: Originally stationed in San Pedro, California, the Fleet was moved to Hawaii in early 1940. The United States wanted to deter Japan's continued expansionist activities in the Pacific, especially in Southeast Asia and the Dutch East Indies. In May 1941, the carrier USS *Yorktown*, a division of Brooklyn-class light cruisers, and about twelve destroyers were unexpectedly detached and ordered to the Atlantic.

Q: **In 1941, what did the American military consider the "Queens of the Seas"?**
    a. Carriers
    b. Battleships
    c. Cruisers

A: Battleships. However, the Japanese believed in carriers. They were superior in tactics and strategy. The Japanese felt carriers might give them the victory they wanted.

Q: **What was Japan's answer should the United States be drawn into hostilities in the Pacific?**

A: From 1909, the Japanese Navy had made the United States Navy its imaginary enemy. During the 1930's, Japan's basic naval strategic plan for dealing with the United States was to let America sortie from Pearl Harbor to make the initial attack. This plan was developed when the United States was numerically superior to the Imperial Combined Fleet. Called "Yogeki Sakusen" or "ambush operations", it called for Japan's powerful submarine fleet to whittle down advancing ships before a final confrontation.

Q: What was Rainbow 5?
A: An ultra-secret United States war plan that if the United States was not attacked by Japan, the United States was to declare war against Japan to protect British and Dutch colonies in the Pacific. It called for the United States Pacific Fleet to capture Japanese positions in the Marshall and Caroline Islands, including Truk, before proceeding to the Philippines. This plan really served a dual purpose. It was Britain's way of getting the United States into Britain's fight with Germany.

Q: Who planned the Hawaii Operation?
A: Rear Admiral Takijro Onishi, Chief of Staff for the Air Fleet. He was an acknowledged air admiral with considerable experience. By early September 1941, Onishi felt the Hawaii Operation seemed too risky and he wanted to recommend to Admiral Yamamoto that it be given up.

Q: Who was considered the "father of Japanese aviation"?
    a. Admiral Isoroku Yamamoto
    b. Rear Admiral Takijro Onishi
    c. Commander Minoru Genda
A: Admiral Yamamoto.

Q: Who planned the attack strategy used at Pearl Harbor?
    a. Admiral Yamamoto
    b. Commander Genda
    c. Commander Fuchida
A: Commander Minoru Genda, a brilliant and daring perfectionist known throughout the Imperial Navy for his tactical expertise in the use of air power.

Commander Minoru Genda, Air Staff Officer,
First Air Fleet. National Archives

Q: What did Commander Minoru Genda use in devising his plan?
A: The thirty-six-year-old tactical adviser had studied the strategies successfully used by the British during its November 12, 1940, attack against the Italian Fleet anchored in Taranto Harbor. He concluded that if 21 British carrier planes could disable three Italian capital ships, Japan's 200 war planes should be able to put most, if not all, of the Pacific Fleet out of commission.

Q: What was the Orange Plan?
A: It was a generic name for a series of naval war plans in the Pacific. In 1941, it basically called for the United States to pull out of the Philippines and attack Japan across the Central Pacific, should Japan begin hostilities with the United States

Q: What was "Operation Z"?
    a. Codename for attack on the Philippines
    b. Codename for the Hawaii Operation
    c. Codename for continued negotiations with the United States
A: The military operation to attack Pearl Harbor was first called "Hawaii Operation." By April 1941, the Pearl Harbor plan had a new name—Operation Z—in honor of the famed "Z" signal given in 1905 by Admiral Heihachiro Togo at Tsushima Straits, where he annihilated the Russian Fleet.

Q: What was the mission of the Hawaiian Department?
A: Its basic mission was two-fold: protection of the Pacific Fleet, and coastal defense of the Hawaiian Islands.

Q: What was the alert system when Lieutenant General Short took command?
A: Major General Charles D. Herron, Short's predecessor, had only one level of alert, total. Short followed a tier alert system to allow time for training.

Q: When did Lieutenant General Short change the alert system in Hawaii?
    a. October 1941
    b. November 1941
    c. December 1941
A: November 5, 1941. In his revised alert system, No. 1 was defense against sabotage; No. 2 was defense against air, surface or submarine attack; and No. 3 was defense against all-out attack. On December 7, Hawaii was on No. 1 alert, the lowest level.

Q: Who was considered the best Navy tactics man?
    a. Admiral Husband Kimmel
    b. Vice Admiral William S. Pye
    c. Vice Admiral William F. Halsey
A: Vice Admiral Pye, Commander, Battle Force and Admiral Kimmel's second-in-command. Kimmel was considered the smartest Navy strategist.

Q: Why did Rear Admiral Bloch have two bosses?
A: As Commandant, 14th Naval District, he was under Admiral Stark, Chief of Naval Operations. As Task Force Commander, he reported to Admiral Kimmel.

Q: When was the last time, before the weekend of December 7, that all the battleships were in port at the same time?
A: July 4, 1941. Kimmel kept much of the fleet in port because he felt Hawaii didn't have enough anti-submarine protection, and intelligence sources regularly reported submarines in the area. However, the battleships were rarely all in port together. Some of the battleships were usually out accompanying Vice Admiral Halsey or Vice Admiral Pye's Task Forces.

Q: What did the United States Navy do that invited attack?
A: It decided to transfer the three American battleships and one carrier to the Atlantic Ocean, leaving eight battleships and three carriers at Pearl Harbor.

Q: What did Admiral Yamamoto admire about the United States?
A: Yamamoto had spent a tour in the United States and had traveled extensively. He had a great appreciation for America's abundant natural resources.

Q: In what ways were Admiral Kimmel and Admiral Yamamoto similar?
A: Both graduated from their country's naval academy in 1904; both were daring, energetic and strongly patriotic. They both had quick tempers. Physically, they were as different as night and day. Kimmel was 5'10" tall and weighed 180 pounds. Yamamoto was 5'3" and weighed about 130 pounds.

Q: What kind of man was Admiral Yamamoto?
A: He was competitive and loved challenges. He was a bold, creative thinker, and unorthodox. He was more broad-minded than most of the officers in the Japanese military and saw that the future was in air power, not battleships.

Q: Why was Admiral Yamamoto called "80sen" by geishas?
A: He had only eight fingers. Two were torn off when a gun he was commanding, while serving aboard the battleship Nisshin during the Russo-Japanese War, exploded.

Q: When was the Japanese First Air Fleet organized?
A: April 10, 1941.

Q: What was "Katamichi Kogeki" or "one way attack"?
A: This plan included flying the carrier planes in from the maximum distance (500-600 miles), attacking, flying back as far as possible, ditching the planes and having the pilots picked up by destroyers or submarines. It was never put into action.

FACT: A radar test was held on November 14, 1941, by the United States Army. It enabled Hawaii to detect carrier planes being launched about 80 miles at sea and to dispatch pursuit aircraft within six minutes to intercept incoming bombers 30 miles from Pearl Harbor.

Q: What was "Genda's Plan"?
A: It was the blueprint for the attack on Pearl Harbor and required that the attack must catch the enemy by surprise; the main objective of the attack

should be United States carriers; another priority should be land-based planes on Oahu; every available carrier should participate in the operation; the attack should utilize all types of bombers: torpedo, dive and high level; fighter planes should play an active part; the attack should be made in daylight, preferably in early morning; refueling at sea would be necessary; all planning must be done in strict secrecy. Genda also recommended an invasion of Hawaii by 10,000 - 15,000 soldiers to secure the island.

Q: When was Vice Admiral Chuichi Nagumo selected to lead the attack force, and by whom was he selected?
    a. Emperor Hirohito
    b. The Naval General Staff
    c. Admiral Yamamoto

A: Nagumo was chosen by the Naval General Staff. He was born on March 25, 1887, in the Yamagata Prefecture in Northern Honshu and graduated among the top ten of his class from Eta Jima Naval Academy. He was designated commander of the Task Force on November 7, 1941, because of his seniority. Military protocol demanded his appointment.

Vice Admiral Chuichi Nagumo, Commander-in-chief, First Air Fleet. National Archives

Q: Did Admiral Yamamoto support an invasion of Hawaii?
A: Admiral Yamamoto wanted containment of the American fleet and air power. The approved plan targeted ships and planes but not shore facilities. Emperor Hirohito had stressed that no civilians were to be hurt. Yamamoto proposed that an expeditionary force come along to occupy Hawaii. However, the army, which ran the government, had no intention of occupying Hawaii.

Q: How was Yamamoto's plan to attack Pearl Harbor transformed from a staff blueprint into a practical plan?
A: Tactical and technical details were ready by September 11, when maneuvers began at the Japanese Naval War College in Tokyo. During ten days of intensive war gaming, only 30 staff officers were allowed in the East Room where charts of Hawaii were laid out. Yamamoto himself supervised those briefings.

Q: When Admiral Yamamoto presented his plan for preemptive strike to Naval headquarters in April, what was the reception?
A: Noncommittal.

Q: The Japanese Naval General Staff fought against the Pearl Harbor attack until what happened?
A: Admiral Yamamoto threatened to resign. Yamamoto was still held to two conditions. First, the Pearl Harbor attack was not to interfere with the Southern Operation and second, nothing would be done to weaken the navy's air strength.

Q: How did Admiral Yamamoto hope the attack would affect the American public?
A: Americans believed that the battleship was the mightiest war weapon. Yamamoto hoped sinking one or more battleships would break the American fighting spirit. Japan felt that knocking out the United States Pacific Fleet in the beginning minutes of the war would demoralize the United States This might give Japan an advantage at the negotiating table.

Q: Why did Japan conduct training exercises at Kagoshima Bay?
A: Because the topography at Kagoshima Bay, including it's shallow depth, was very similar to Pearl Harbor's depth of 45 feet.

Q: The biggest potential headache the Japanese navy had in preparing for the attack on Pearl Harbor was how to use their most deadly and effective weapon against warships, the torpedo, in the shallow waters of the harbor. How was this solved?
A: Wooden stabilizers were fitted on the fins of the torpedoes which kept them from hitting the bottom of Pearl Harbor. The Japanese pilots practiced at Kagoshima Bay in early November, in anticipation of the attack on Pearl Harbor. The carrier pilots found that by flying almost at sea level and releasing the refitted torpedoes low over the water, and then banking steeply immediately afterwards to clear the target, they were able to hit their targets eight times out of ten.

Q: How did Germany's actions in Europe affect Japan's decision to attack?
A: Germany attacked the Soviet Union and seemed the victor in the late fall of '41. With Russia occupied, Japan felt it was time to move against the United States

Q: How were the Japanese operational units organized?
A: The Hawaii Operation was divided into two units. One was the Task Force, which was responsible for the aerial attacks. The second unit was the submarine force. It was responsible for submarine attacks.

Q: When did Admiral Nagumo announce to the Task Force that their mission was to attack Pearl Harbor?
A: Nagumo outlined their mission at a special conference held aboard the carrier Akagi on the morning of November 23. All his commanding officers and staff from every ship were present.

Q: What was the Model SCR-270?
A: A mobile early warning radar with a maximum range of 150 miles. The Americans were just starting to use radar.

Q: How were oscilloscopes used as warning devices?
A: They could register visual echoes of planes picked up for a maximum effective distance of 130 miles.

Q: What problem between the signal corps and the interceptor command of the air corps helped Japan execute the surprise attack?
A: Major General Frederick Martin, commander of the Hawaiian Air Force, asked Lieutenant General Short several times to place Short's radio sections under Martin's command so that Martin could coordinate the efforts of radio operators with his combat planes. Short refused, deciding that signal officers would control the radio sections until radio operators were properly trained.

Q: The four principle radar mobile stations on Oahu were located at Opana, Kaaawa, Kawailoa and Koko Head. Where was the back-up station?
        a. Fort Shafter
        b. Aliamanu Crater
        c. Schofield Barracks
A: Fort Shafter.

FACT: The two-man midget submarines practiced making submerged attacks off the rocky coast of Shikoku, smallest of Japan's main islands. They were finally accepted as a valuable part of the Task Force on October 9, only after participating in a full rehearsal with the battleship *Nagato* in Hiroshima Bay.

Q: When did radar warning units on Oahu become operational?
        a. July 1940
        b. January 1941
        c. November 1941
A: November 14, 1941.

Q: What was one of the United States Navy's biggest mistakes?
A: They prepared for submarine rather than aerial attack. Rear Admiral Bloch and Admiral Kimmel didn't believe that aerial torpedoes could be used in Pearl Harbor because of the depth of the water. Bloch knew the bombs were very destructive but he did not think that they could penetrate decks and get into the machinery parts, despite the fact that, in June 1941, Hawaii was notified that Pearl Harbor's shallow water was no longer a protection from torpedo attacks.

Q: What was the "winds message"?
A: On November 19, 1941, American signal stations intercepted two messages, the second repeating the first: "Regarding the broadcast of a special message in an emergency. In case of emergency (danger of cutting of our diplomatic relations), and the cutting off of international communications, the following warning will be added in the middle of the daily Japanese language short-wave news broadcast. 1. In case of Japan-US relations in dan-

ger: *Higashi no kazeame* (east wind rain) 2. Japan-USSR relations: *Kitano-kaze kumoni* (north wind cloudy) 3. Japan-British relations: *Nishi no kaze hare* (west wind clear)...when this is heard please destroy all codes, etc."

Q: **Why was the attack on December 7?**
A: There were several reasons. First, to coincide with the beginning of air raids and landings in Malaya. Second, to improve chances that the bulk of the United States fleet would be in port. Third, to take advantage of the moon cycle which would provide maximum moonlight for night operations. Japan had other non-strategic reasons. Stocks of war material, principally oil, were dwindling and the United States was growing stronger each day in the Pacific. Continued delay would weaken rather than strengthen Japan's fighting capability.

Q: **What was strange about Vice Admiral Nagumo's appointment as commander of the Japanese Task Force?**
A: Nagumo never served aboard a carrier until he took command of the First Air Fleet. He used text book summaries of naval air warfare techniques.

Q: **Why was Vice Admiral Nagumo strongly against the attack on Pearl Harbor?**
A: He believed the only result would be stiff retaliation from the United States.

Q: **Admiral Yamamoto disliked the timid Vice Admiral Nagumo. Why didn't he replace him?**
A: Yamamoto believed replacing Nagumo might have had an adverse effect on the morale of the whole fleet.

Q: **On November 26, 1941, what did Army Chief of Staff General George C. Marshall, ask the commander of the Army Air Corps to do?**
A: Anticipating war with Japan, General Marshall directed General "Hap" Arnold to make a study and prepare for "general incendiary attacks" to burn up the wood and paper structures of the densely populated Japanese cities.

Q: **On November 28, what message did the Chief of Naval Operations, Admiral Stark, send to Admiral Kimmel?**
A: Admiral Stark told him that negotiations with Japan appeared to have ended and that, in the event hostilities could not be avoided, the United States wanted the Japanese to strike first.

Q: **On November 28, Admiral Kimmel gave an order that put the United States Pacific Fleet on a "war footing". What was it?**
A: Kimmel ordered that all submerged submarines operating in the restricted waters around Pearl Harbor were to be considered hostile and should be fired upon. Orders were also given to Vice Admiral Halsey, who was on board the aircraft carrier USS *Enterprise* enroute to Wake Island to deliver aircraft, "to sink any Japanese vessel he finds".

Q: The Americans believed that if Japan launched an attack on Pearl Harbor, what type of an attack would it be?
    a. Air
    b. Naval bombardment
    c. Submarine

A: Submarine. Despite that belief, the Army and Navy periodically conducted "dog fights" and mock raids on Sunday mornings and dropped water-filled bombs on the USS *Utah* for practice.

Q: What type of attack did the military in Washington, D.C. believe would be used against Hawaii?
    a. An invasion
    b. A diversionary attack
    c. A commando attack

A: All believed that a major attack would happen in the Pacific, but it would most likely occur in the Philippines. They felt that any attack on Hawaii would be strictly diversionary.

Q: Admiral Husband Kimmel, CINCUS, doubted the possibility of a carrier attack. Why?
    a. He believed that Japan would never attack the United States
    b. Japanese carriers were made for only short range excursions
    c. Japan didn't have the strength in carriers to pull off such an excursion.

A: The answer is b. Apparently Kimmel did not take into account that the Japanese also had fuel tankers.

Q: Why didn't Admiral Kimmel put torpedo nets around the ships moored at Pearl Harbor?

A: Despite all the warnings, Kimmel decided the nets would restrict the ships if he had to have the congested harbor cleared in an emergency.

Q: When did Emperor Hirohito's Imperial Conference decide Japan should declare war against the United States?
    a. January 15, 1941
    b. June 9, 1941
    c. December 1, 1941
    d. December 6, 1941

A: The answer is c. The conference participants urged war. Hirohito's silent acceptance of war counsel signaled his acceptance of the conflict.

Emperor Hirohito. National Archives

Q: When did Admiral Yamamoto receive the Imperial Rescript Order to lead the Japanese Combined Fleet into war?
        a. At 1700 December 2
        b. At 0915 December 5
        c. At 0755 December 7
A: At a formal audience with the Emperor at 1700 December 2.

Q: What was the military population in Hawaii in December 1941?
        a. 10,000
        b. 15,000
        c. 25,000
A: Twenty-five thousand.

Q: What air base was considered home for the Hawaiian Air Force?
        a. Wheeler
        b. Haleiwa
        c. Hickam
A: Hickam.

INTELLIGENCE

Q: What was OP-20-G?
A: This was the title given the Code and Signal Section of the United States Naval Communication Service on its reorganization in July 1922. It was headed by Lieutenant Lawrence F. Safford.

Q: What was JAP?
    a. A Japanese
    b. An encoding device made by the Japanese
    c. A radio transmitter
A: Operating at 11,980 kilocycles, it was Japan's most powerful transmitter.

Q: What was a major problem in the United States military's handling of intelligence?
A: The Navy's OP-20-G and the Army's Signal Intelligence Service worked separately and very seldom shared information with each other.

Q: When did OP-20-G receive its first complete translation of a Japanese diplomatic message from Tokyo?
A: 12 June 1920.

Q: Who was considered by many to be the world's most famous code-breaker?
    a. William Friedman
    b. Herbert O. Yardley
    c. Lawrence F. Safford
A: Yardley, born April 13, 1889, became a commissioned officer in 1916 and set up Section 8 of United States Military Intelligence (MI-8), America's first code-breaking agency. Yardley was recruited after he wrote "Solution of America's Diplomatic Codes", which showed America's codes were very insecure.

Q: What was the SIS?
    a. The British Secret Intelligence Service
    b. The United States Army Signal Intelligence Service
    c. The United States Secret Intelligence Service
A: The United States Army's Signal Intelligence Service.

FACT: The Navy originally handled both Japanese diplomatic and naval messages. It was the only de-crypting agency for the State Department. In 1930, when the Army's SIS was created, the Army began work on the Japanese diplomatic messages and eventually took over the entire task, leaving OP-20-G free to concentrate on naval traffic.

Q: What was ONI?
    a. The United States Navy Office of Naval Intelligence
    b. The British Office of Intelligence
    c. An acronym for Japan's intelligence
A: The Office of Naval Intelligence.

Q: What was the Underwood Code Machine?
A: Resembling a regular Underwood typewriter, it had Japanese characters which resembled kana characters in Japanese brush stokes. The machine was built in 1924, at the request of Lieutenant Safford. It let operators listening to Morse code signals press the English letter key board and have the kana brush stroke print on the paper. Although the keyboard took care of only 26 of the 73 kana characters, it helped reduce training time for the operators.

Q: When was the first Purple message intercepted by the United States Army Signal Intelligence Service?
A: The first message intercepted was from Tokyo to Berlin in March 1939.

Q: In May of 1939, the Americans learned that the Japanese had introduced a new code system. What was it called?
    a. JN-25
    b. Navy Code "D"
    c. NIP
A: The Japanese called it "Navy Code D"; United States intelligence called it JN-25. The Americans discovered in November 1939 that the code system used for JN-25 had been used by the American Army and Navy in the Spanish-American War in 1898 and later by both the British and French

navies in World War I. The United States abandoned it in 1917 because it was considered insecure.

FACT: American codebreakers used an electrical device to decode diplomatic cipher messages sent between the Japanese Foreign Ministry and their diplomats stationed around the world. It was invented by William Friedman, chief cryptanalyst of the United States Army Signal Corps. The name given to this device was the "Purple Machine". By custom, OP-20-G assigned color code names to the various code machines.

Q: The Japanese Navy Secret Operation Code-1918, with updates through 1929, was known as Code B, but was more commonly called the "Red Book". The new code adopted as the General Naval Code in 1930 was known as the "Blue Book." Why were the two called "Red" and "Blue"?
    a. Nicknames of the agents that broke the codes
    b. Books were kept in red and blue leather binders
    c. Codes were named after colors in the American flag
A: The names given the books were from the color of the binders in which they were kept. Some of the information obtained in the books was obtained from burglaries by ONI.

Q: In July 1922, the United States Navy Communication Service was reorganized and Lieutenant Lawrence F. Safford was named the head of the new division, OP-20-G. Who taught him the principles of codebreaking?
    a. Herbert O. Yardley
    b. Alwyn D. Kramer
    c. Agnes Driscoll
A: One of America's most brilliant codebreakers, Agnes Driscoll. She was qualified in four languages, German, French, Latin and Japanese; she also had incredible mathematical skills. Safford was her "student" in 1924.

Q: What happened to Lieutenant Safford?
A: By 1941, he had been promoted to Commander Safford and, at the time of the attack on Pearl Harbor, he was head of the Navy's Communications Division, Security (Intelligence) Section in Washington, D.C.

FACT: The United States Navy had been in the codebreaking business from 1899. During World War I it concentrated on establishing a network of medium-frequency direction-finding (DF) stations along the East Coast to track German submarines operating in the Western Atlantic.

Q: How did JN-25 differ from J-19?
A: JN-25 was the Japanese Navy operational code and J-19 was Japan's high-level diplomatic code.

Q: Who were Agnes Meyer, "Wimpy" Currier and Philip Cate?
A: Along with Agnes Driscoll, they worked in the Security Section of the Navy's Communication Division (OP-20-G) and were the "first team" of the navy's codebreakers.

Q: What was "magic" and "ultra"?
    a. Names referred to cryptanalysts
    b. Codenames for the American President and the Japanese Emperor
    c. Names given to two Japanese "spies" in Honolulu
A: These two names referred to the American and British cryptanalysts; the Americans because they were "magicians" in decoding messages and the British because their operation was "ultra-secret".

Q: What was the Japanese encoding device called?
    a. The Alphabetical Typewriter
    b. The Radio Encoder
    c. The Crypto Writer
A: Developed by Captain Risaburo Ito in 1937 as an improvement of the Type 91 cryptograph or Red machine, it was called the Alphabetical Typewriter. The Japanese called it their Type B machine while the United States called it M-J, then B machine, and finally codename Purple.

Q: What was "Hypo"?
    a. A decoding machine
    b. An intelligence unit
    c. A radio relay station
A: Station Hypo, located in Pearl Harbor, was the Fourteenth Naval District's communications intelligence unit. One of its missions was to breakdown the Japanese officer system.

Q: What important role did Commander Joseph J. Rochefort play in American intelligence?
    a. He was the Fourteenth Naval District's intelligence officer
    b. He was Admiral Kimmel's intelligence officer
    c. He headed the Pearl Harbor Intelligence Unit
A: Commander Rochefort was the head of the Pearl Harbor Intelligence Unit. Captain Irving Mayfield was the Fourteenth Naval District's intelligence officer and Lieutenant Commander Edwin T. Layton was Admiral Kimmel's intelligence officer.

Q: On November 3, 1941, Commander Rochefort, whose Combat Intelligence Unit at Pearl Harbor had been tracking Japanese carriers, noted a new address called "First Air Fleet." What did he miss?
A: He never imagined that the new Japanese unit identified was the organization which would eventually attack Pearl Harbor. It was conducting a full-scale practice for Operation Hawaii.

FACT: "Magic" allowed the United States to translate Japanese codes for a long time. As events escalated toward war, the United States continually monitored the information transmitted to and from Japan. A major drawback to the United States easy access to information was that there were many "false alarms." Consequently, "war looming" messages had less and less impact. That contributed to the casual way message traffic about Pearl Harbor was treated.

Q: Japanese Naval Intelligence, Third Bureau, was run by whom?
A: Captain Kanji Ogawa, a former assistant naval attache once assigned to Washington, D.C.

Q: Who was Lieutenant Commander Itaru Tachibana?
A: A brothel keeper in Los Angeles. He was identified as a spy for Japan through United States counter-intelligence operations. Instead of standing trial, he was invited to leave as a diplomatic concession to Japanese-American relations, an action that would be regretted later. One of Captain Kanji Ogawa's principle assistants, Tachibana played a leading role in assembling detailed intelligence that made the attack on Pearl Harbor possible.

FACT: A model of Pearl Harbor was constructed at the Imperial Naval College in Tokyo. First, a bare outline of the harbor was created. Then, as more information was obtained about the Fleet's movements in and out of the harbor, miniatures of the United States ships were created to scale and placed in the last-known location of the original ships.

Japanese detail model of Pearl Harbor. National Archives

Q: Whose duty was it to keep the United States Army in Hawaii informed about United States naval intelligence?
    a. Army Signal Corps
    b. Rear Admiral Bloch, Commander Fourteenth Naval District
    c. Rear Admiral Richmond Turner, Director of War Plans
A: Rear Admiral Bloch. Unfortunately, Bloch was too complacent and it resulted in the military command ignoring the Navy Department's warning on April 1, 1941, that the Axis nations tended to attack on Saturdays, Sundays and national holidays. The November 27, 1941, message, which was to

put Hawaii on "a full war footing", resulted in Bloch instructing the Coast Guard to conduct submarine surveillance along the coastline. The "war message" was retransmitted through Navy channels on November 28. It was still not understood or acted upon. Ironically, Hawaii is the only place that apparently misunderstood.

Q: Why didn't Hawaii routinely monitor commercial messages sent between Japan and the Japanese Consulate in Honolulu?
A: Captain Irving Mayfield, the Fourteenth Naval District's intelligence officer, tried for a long time to circumvent the Federal Communications Act of 1934 and get copies of the protected communications between the Japanese Consul General in Hawaii and the Foreign Office in Tokyo. The Act forbade commercial communication companies from disclosing to anyone, other than the addressee, the contents of messages. In November, Mayfield persuaded David Sarnoff, president of Radio Corporation of America (RCA), to have file copies of Japanese messages sent to him. The first batch came in less than a week before the attack on Pearl Harbor.

Q: Why was Bainbridge Island, Washington, so important to the United States Navy?
A: It was that naval station which intercepted messages between Tokyo and its ambassadors in Washington, D.C.

Q: What was the *Taiyo Maru* and what important role did it play in the Pearl Harbor attack?
A: A passenger ocean liner, it sailed from Japan in October 1941 to make a trial run of Vice Admiral Nagumo's future course, checking the weather, distance traveled, visibility, wind directions and velocity, pitch and roll of the ship, and sea conditions. It docked in Honolulu on a Sunday morning to observe the harbor traffic.

Q: Once the *Taiyo Maru* docked in Honolulu, how did the Japanese consulate members pass military information to the ship?
A: Newspapers were delivered daily to the ship. Inside the bundles were memorandums and secret slips of paper with information on the United States Fleet's training maneuvers and weekend habits, size of the air force and exact location of installations.

Q: When the *Taiyo Maru* was in port, the Federal Bureau of Investigation (FBI), the Army Intelligence (G2) and Customs all watched the activities between the Japanese Consulate and the ship. Why was the information passed so easily?
A: All the agencies were more occupied with passengers than routine deliveries.

Q: How did the Japanese analyze weather conditions over Hawaii?
A: Detailed weather reports of the islands and the surrounding areas appeared daily in the Honolulu press.

Q: In the months prior to the attack, what was the concern of Hawaii's top army and navy personnel about the "Fifth Column"?
A: They were concerned about possible sabotage by local Japanese. Army intelligence estimated that a sizeable number of local males of Japanese origin had organized and they were prepared to attack objectives on Oahu, especially the navy installations. Military wives were repeatedly warned that the local Japanese might rise up and massacre American women and children.

Q: What was Japan's most valuable source of information about the activities going on in Hawaii?
    a. American radio traffic
    b. The Japanese Consulate in Honolulu
    c. Local newspapers
A: The Japanese Consulate in Honolulu. Its espionage network gave Japan a constant flow of current information. The official diplomatic list of the Honolulu Japanese Consulate showed only five associate consuls. According to naval intelligence and FBI reports, there were more than 200 sub-consulars scattered throughout the Hawaiian Islands.

Q: What valuable information was provided by the Japanese Consulate about the fleet?
A: The fleet either went out on Tuesday and returned on Friday or went out on Friday and returned on Saturday of the next week. In either case, it stayed in the harbor about a week. When it went out for two weeks, it would usually return by Sunday. The fleet trained to the southeast of Pearl Harbor.

Q: How did the Japanese Strike Force identify the United States Fleet's exercise area?
A: Intercepted radio messages from planes flying between the training area and Pearl Harbor showed that the planes were flying for forty to sixty minutes. The training area was estimated to be near Maui. It was hard to determine whether the fleet put in to any other port during training periods and, if so, where. There were some indications that it might go to Lahaina or Maalaea for a short period of time.

Q: What role did Takeo Yoshikawa play in the attack on Pearl Harbor?
A: Yoshikawa, a Japanese naval intelligence agent, was sent to Hawaii after four years of training in English and espionage techniques. He arrived in Honolulu on March 20, 1941, under the alias Tadashi Morimura, and worked as a clerk in the Japanese Consulate. With a keen eye, he kept track of the military activities on Oahu. His discovery of the lack of air patrols off northern Oahu was a key factor in the planning of the Pearl Harbor attack.

Q: Who was the "sleeper spy"?
A: Bernard Julius Otto Kuehn, who lived in Hawaii for several years posing as an owner of a furniture business. He was a member of the German navy's secret police and was under contract with Japan's navy from 1935. The Japanese, who called him "Ichiro Fujii", mis-trusted Kuehn's ability to do the job. He was considered too nervous and jumpy, and had a reputation as a "money eater". The information he gave was considered useless.

FACT: In March 1939, Captain Ogawa, head of Japanese Intelligence, Third Bureau, stopped off in Honolulu and gave Kuehn a special designed portable radio transmitter. A "quickly devised" radio, it could fit in a suit case. Kuehn was told to lie low. If war came between Japan and the United States, Kuehn was to use the equipment to send messages to Japanese subs waiting off Oahu. The subs would relay the messages to Japan. By 1938 or early 1939, Fourteenth Naval District intelligence officers spotted Kuehn as a probable agent for Germany or Japan, or both.

Q: Who or what was "Tricycle"?
A: He was a British double agent named Dusko Popov. He reported to the FBI on August 11, 1941, that he had been directed by German officials to go to Hawaii to locate ammunition dumps and airfields on the island of Oahu and gather information about Pearl Harbor. The FBI ignored his information because the Director, J. Edgar Hoover, didn't like Popov's reputation as "a ladies man" who enjoyed two women at a time, hence his name.

Q: In the Fall of 1941, Eric Sevareid, a newsman for Columbia Broadcast System (CBS), was told that Japan was going to attack Pearl Harbor before Christmas. Where did that information come from?
A: Kilsoo Haan, an agent from the Sino-Korean People's League, made that report based on information from his friends in Korea.

Q: What was the famous "bomb message"?
A: On September 24, 1941, Japan directed the Japanese Consulate in Honolulu to provide specific information about the ships at Pearl Harbor, by type and class; which were anchored and which were tied up at wharfs, buoys and in dry docks; and when were more than one ship alongside the same dock. Although the army in Washington, D.C. translated it by October 9, 1941, no one passed the message on to the Hawaii commanders. No one in the War Plans Division, headed by Brigadier General Gerow, thought it was important.

Q: When Captain H. D. Bode, head of the United States Navy's Foreign Intelligence, and Captain Kirk, Chief of Office of Naval Intelligence, learned of the "bomb message", they urged that the Navy send the message to Admiral Kimmel. What happened to them?
A: A few days after they argued with Rear Admiral Turner, Director of War Plans (OP-12), to send the message, both were detached from their intelligence assignments and placed elsewhere.

FACT: On November 15, the Honolulu Consulate reported to Tokyo that "ships in harbor depart irregular but at a rate of twice a week." The United States Navy didn't translate this important message until December 3, 1941. Washington paid little attention, not even informing Admiral Kimmel or Lieutenant General Short.

Q: How did the Japanese convince the United States intelligence that the Japanese ships were still in Japanese water?
A: The regular carrier operators stayed behind, at Kure Naval Station, and sent

fake messages to other ships as if they were still on their carriers. Since a wireless operator's touch is very distinctive, hearing the familiar rhythms continued the deception that the fleet was still in home water.

Q: **Why was it impossible for the American intelligence units at Pearl Harbor to track the Japanese carriers that were heading toward them?**
A: Vice Admiral Nagumo took no chances on being detected. He had all crystals removed from radios to ensure radio silence was maintained. Nagumo would not even permit garbage to be thrown overboard. The battleship *Hiei* had the best radio reception and transmitted information to the other vessels by blinker and signal flags.

Q: **Why wasn't Admiral Kimmel alarmed by the message intercepted by the Purple Team?**
A: Ironically, purple intercepted messages were not sent to Kimmel. Nor did he have a purple machine in Hawaii. A request was made for one but the Office of Naval Intelligence felt it was unnecessary because most of the information were political and they didn't think the military had a need to know since they couldn't do anything about politics. Eight were constructed. Four were kept in Washington, D.C., one in the Philippines and three in London.

Q: **Was the message "East-wind-rain" ever sent?**
A: An officer with the Australian Special Intelligence Organization, near Melbourne, reported hearing the message on December 4, while monitoring the Japanese news broadcast from Tokyo. Ralph Briggs, senior operator with the United States Navy, also identified the message at Chelton Station and telephoned it to OP-20-G in Washington. Lieutenant Commander Kramer received it in Washington and Captain Safford noted that Kramer had seen it and sent a copy to Rear Admiral Leigh Noyes.

FACT: On December 3, the Office of Naval Intelligence told the naval attaches at Tokyo, Peking, Bangkok and Shanghai to destroy all their codes, ciphers, secret and confidential material. When the attaches were prepared, they were to send ONI the code word, "Gobbledygook." By this action, the top American naval commanders in those areas were alerted that Americans were getting ready for hostilities, although there was no announcement that Pearl Harbor might be attacked or that war was imminent.

Q: **Were reports made to intelligence officers on the presence of Japanese carriers in the Pacific?**
A: Yes. One was from the SS *Lurline.* Another was made by a Dutch official who had learned the carriers' location. Kilsoo Haan gave another warning on December 3, that an air attack would probably occur on a Sunday, a day of rest for the American Fleet. One Netherlands' official, Captain Johan E. Ranneft, recorded that when he visited the United States Office of Naval Intelligence on December 2, the United States Navy already knew the location of the Japanese carriers. The ships were posted on a map in the office. None of this information was passed to Admiral Kimmel.

AS ZERO HOUR APPROACHES
(Nov 26 - Dec 6)

Q: **What is the distance between Japan and Hawaii?**
    a. 3,394 miles
    b. 2,249 miles
    c. over 4,000 miles
A: 3,394 miles.

Q: **What was "Kido Butai"?**
A: Japan named the Task Force it sent to Hawaii "Kido Butai", or "Strike Force".

Q: **Why was the attack to be at Pearl Harbor?**
A: Japan considered the Pacific Fleet to be a dagger at its throat and was committed to fight. The American Fleet was more likely to be at its home port than anywhere else.

Q: **Where was the assembly area for the Japanese Task Force?**
A: By November 22, the entire force had gathered at Hitokappu Bay on Etorofu, the second-most southern island of the Kurile Islands, a chain extending northeast from Hokkaido.

Q: Who was the commander of the Task Force and what was his flagship?
- a. Admiral Isoroku Yamamoto, battleship *Nagato*
- b. Vice Admiral Chuichi Nagumo, the carrier *Akagi*
- c. Rear Admiral Tamon Yamaguchi, the carrier *Soryu*

A: Nagumo commanded the Task Force sailing for Hawaii; his flag ship was the *Akagi*. Yamamoto was the commander-in-chief of the Combined Fleet. Yamaguchi was the commander of the Second Carrier Division with Nagumo.

Q: What were the first Japanese navy units to depart in strength for Hawaii?
- a. Submarines
- b. Battleships
- c. Carriers

A: Submarines, which left 10 days before the rest of the Task Force.

Q: When did the Japanese Task Force sail for Hawaii?
- a. November 20
- b. November 26
- c. December 1

A: In the early morning of November 26, 1941, in a thick fog, the Task Force set sail for Pearl Harbor.

Q: Why were the submarines sent ahead of the Task Force?
A: Twenty-five submarines left ahead of the Task Force and positioned themselves around Hawaii and between Hawaii and the west coast of the United States to finish off any crippled ships limping back to the west coast for repairs after the attack. Five of them were "mother" ships, carrying the mini-subs.

Q: What did the Japanese Task Force consist of?
A: Six carriers, eleven destroyers, two battleships, two heavy cruisers, one light cruiser, three submarines and eight supporting tankers.

Q: How many air groups were aboard the carriers?
- a. 15
- b. 22
- c. 26

A: Twenty-six.

Q: What were the total number of planes in the Japanese Task Force?
- a. 172
- b. 311
- c. 423

A: Four hundred and twenty-three.

Q: The Task Force was built around three carrier divisions. Which carriers made up the First, Second and Fifth Division?
A: The *Shokaku* and *Zuikaku* made up the Fifth Division, the *Soryu* and *Hiryu* were the Second Division, and the carriers *Akagi* and *Kaga* were the First Division.

Q: **How many planes were assigned to each carrier?**
A: The *Akagi* and *Kaga* each carried 18 fighters, 18 dive bombers and 27 high-level or torpedo bombers. The *Shokaku* and *Zuikaku* each carried 18 fighters, 27 dive bombers and 27 high-level bombers. The *Soryu* and *Hiryu* each had 18 fighters, 18 dive bombers and 18 high-level bombers.

Q: **What did the Task Force do to conserve fuel?**
A: The ships were operating on minimum power. They were unheated and dimly lighted, in efforts to help conserve fuel. The destroyers required daily refueling. The carriers stored additional fuel in barrels on their decks. Many of them returned with their fuel almost exhausted.

FACT: As the Task Force traveled toward Hawaii, its usual formation was destroyers in the front, followed by the two heavy cruisers. The six carriers were stationed in the center, traveling in two columns. Three of the original 28 submarines intended as advance scouts stayed in the center because of the poor visibility. The remaining ships were scattered throughout the formation. Two battleships brought up the rear. Sailing speed was set by the slowest ship, the tanker *Toei Maru*. The Task Force traveled at 12 to 14 knots, slowing to nine knots for refueling. On the final leg, the Task Force left the slow-moving tankers behind and made a rush to the launching point. Speed was essential. Bucket brigades were formed to fuel the engines.

Q: **In the winter months the Northern Pacific Ocean has very bad weather and rough seas. Why was this northern route taken on the Japanese approach to Hawaii?**
    a. It was the shortest route
    b. Better concealment
    c. It was easier to escape if spotted
A: Concealment. In the winter months the Americans very seldom used the northern route. The Americans believed that the Japanese would not risk this approach.

Q: **Next to secrecy, what was the number-two concern on the Japanese priority list?**
    a. Refueling the ships on the voyage
    b. Weather
    c. Locating the United States carriers
A: Because of the harsh weather in the Northern Pacific, refueling the ships on the voyage.

Q: **What happened at Pearl Harbor on November 28, that aroused suspicion?**
A: The cruiser USS *Helena* spotted an unidentified submarine operating in the restricted sea area just outside Pearl Harbor.

Q: **How did the Americans keep track of Japanese warships?**
    a. Their spy network
    b. By radio traffic
    c. By submarine reconnaissance
A: By radio traffic.

Q: As the Task Force sailed for Hawaii, where was the main body of the combined fleet?
A: With Admiral Yamamoto in the Inland Sea, prepared to protect the Japanese homeland. This great bulk was at sea as of December 1, ready for war.

Q: What was the mission for the Imperial Fifth Fleet?
A: Commanded by Vice Admiral Hoshiro Hosogaya, it was to protect and defend waters east of Japan, and to guard the route of the Pearl Harbor attack force.

Q: What were the Japanese prepared to lose in the attack?
A: The attack was so important, the Japanese General Staff was prepared to lose two or three carriers.

Q: What chance of success did the Japanese General Staff believe the Task Force had of making a surprise attack?
    a. 20%
    b. 40%
    c. 100%
A: Forty percent.

Q: What four main problems concerned Vice Admiral Nagumo as he sailed toward Hawaii?
A: First, the possibility of being discovered en route; second, the state of alertness on Oahu; third, the chance of finding the fleet in Pearl Harbor; and fourth, the probability of United States retaliation.

Q: What was one of the fears the commanders of the Japanese carriers had about their submarines?
A: That the subs would trigger a premature action, thus taking away the chance of a surprise attack and possibly jeopardizing the whole Task Force.

Q: If the Japanese Task Force was discovered en route to Pearl Harbor, what was it to do?
A: If the Task Force was sighted before X day minus 2, they were to abandon the operation and return to Japan. If it was one day before X day, it was left up to the discretion of the Task Force commander whether to reverse course or launch the attack.

Q: What does "Climb Mt. Niitaka 1208,1208" mean?
A: Admiral Yamamoto sent this message to the fleet on November 30. It meant "proceed with attack as planned on 08 December", December 7, in Hawaii.

Q: Why didn't radio silence from the Japanese during the week prior to December 7, bother Admiral Kimmel?
A: During the previous six months, there were 12 separate periods, ranging from 9-22 days, or a total of 134 days, when locations of Japanese carriers from radio traffic were uncertain.

Q: Why did the luxury liner SS Lurline delay its scheduled noon departure from Honolulu on Friday December 5?
A: Hundreds of military dependents were booked for that voyage and they were still arriving after dark. The Lurline set sail for San Francisco after midnight.

Q: Why did the December 6 message, sent from the submarine I-72 that the American Fleet was not in Lahaina, dash Japan's hopes?
A: The Lahaina anchorage was used for training because it was open and deep. If the fleet had been there, the Japanese felt that they had their best chance for success.

Q: On the evening of December 6, what did Admiral Kimmel wisely turn down?
A: An invitation to cocktails at the Japanese Consulate.

Q: In the hours preceding the attack, what did Vice Admiral Nagumo rely on to tell him if the Americans were alert to their presence?
A: He listened to a Honolulu radio station. He felt if the Americans were on alert, the radio would make that announcement. All he heard was Hawaiian music.

Q: What percentage of the fleet was on shore leave on the evening of December 6?
    a. About one-third
    b. A little over one-half
    c. Three-fourths
A: About one-third of all ships' crews were on pass. Shore leave expired at midnight on December 7.

Q: With the alerts and the tense conditions in the Pacific, why did Admiral Kimmel allow leave time?
A: Morale was becoming a major problem. Kimmel was trying to relieve some of the strain on his men because of family separation and the intensive training schedule. He demanded that more facilities be provided ashore, especially for enlisted men's recreation.

Q: What part did the *Lanikai* play in the war?
A: The *Lanikai* was a two-masted, 75-ton auxiliary schooner. It was commissioned as a United States naval vessel on December 5, 1941. It was supposed to be a lure, encouraging attack by the Japanese. The "cover" story was that it was looking for the crew of a downed plane. The actual mission was to patrol off Camranh Bay and report Japanese Fleet movements. The *Lanikai* was anchored south of Java when the attack began on Pearl Harbor.

Q: On the evening of December 6, Pearl Harbor conducted a contest called "Battle of the Bands". Which ship won?
    a. USS Arizona
    b. USS Oklahoma
    c. USS Pennsylvania
A: USS Pennsylvania.

FACT: On the evening of December 6, a Lieutenant and a Seaman First Class at the Twelfth Naval District in San Francisco had tracked the *Kido Butai* to a position approximately four hundred miles north-northwest of Oahu. There was no doubt that Pearl Harbor was going to be raided the next morning.

ATTACK ON PEARL HARBOR

Q: **At what time did the midget submarines detach from the class "I" "mother" ship?**
A: They were launched between seven-and-one-half to twelve miles from Pearl Harbor between 0100 and a little after 0330 on December 7.

Q: **What defect appeared after the midget subs were launched?**
A: Faulty communications systems. All but one lost contact with their "mother" submarines after launching.

Q: **How large were the midget submarines?**
A: They measured 45 feet long and 12 feet from the top of the conning tower to the bottom of the hull. They held a crew of two and were armed with two torpedoes. The subs were stored in large tubes on the decks of the "mother" subs. Each had an underwater speed of 19 knots.

FACT: The battle plan for the midget subs was to detach from the "mother" submarines several miles off-shore, slip into Pearl Harbor and wait for the air attack to begin before commencing their own action. They were to strike between the first and second waves. If necessary, they were to wait until nightfall to attack, then circle around Ford Island to escape the harbor.

Q: **Was the first Japanese/American contact on December 7, the aerial attack?**
A: No. The mine sweeper *Condor* spotted what looked like a submarine's wake at 0342 on December 7. She notified the destroyer USS *Ward*, which searched unsuccessfully for the submarine for approximately an hour.

Q: **What did the Japanese heavy cruisers *Tone* and *Chikuma* do at approximately 0530 on December 7?**
A: Each sent aloft a single-engine reconnaissance plane. The plane from the *Tone* was to check the Lahaina anchorage, then proceed south of Pearl Harbor in search of American ships. The *Chikuma's* plane was to check weather conditions and make a last-minute report of the ships at Pearl Harbor.

Q: **Before launching their planes the Japanese were worried that an American patrol plane might spot them. Were any planes seen?**
A: Luck was still with the aggressor. For days, the dawn patrol of American PBYs had flown southward, almost 180-degrees in the opposite direction.

Q: **How did the *Akagi* give the signal for the planes to take off?**
A: The carrier flew a set of flags at half-mast, which meant "get ready." When the flags were hoisted to the top and then quickly lowered, that was the signal for the planes to begin taking off.

Japanese dive bombers warming up on the flight deck. National Archives

Q: **How far from Oahu was the Japanese Task Force when it launched its planes?**
    a. Approximately 415 miles
    b. Approximately 230 miles
    c. Approximately 100 miles

A: The launching occurred approximately 230 miles north of Oahu.

Q: **What did almost every officer and crewman in the attacking force do before taking off?**
A: Many tied "hachimakis" or traditional white clothes around their heads. This signified one was embarking on a project of great moment requiring courage and determination. Most had marked their head wear with the symbol of the rising sun and the legend "sure victory."

Q: **Vice Admiral Nagumo planned to hit Pearl Harbor with 356 planes sent out in two waves. How many planes did he keep aboard the carriers to guard the fleet?**
    a. 26
    b. 39
    c. 47
A: Thirty-nine fighters were left to guard the Task Force in case the Americans struck back.

Q: **What type of planes did the Japanese use in their attack on Pearl Harbor?**
A: The fighters were Mitsubushi A6M2 Type 00 Zero-sen, known to the Americans as the "Zero". The dive-bombers were the Aichi D3A1 Type 99. They were also known as "Val"s. Both the high-level and torpedo bombers were the Nakajima B5N2 Type 97. Those planes were called "Kate"s.

Q: **Why did the Japanese launch their attack in two waves?**
A: Although one massive attack would have been preferable to maximize the surprise element and maximize the damage, the Japanese decided to use two waves because it would take too long for all the planes to become airborne as one group. The first planes aloft would waste too much fuel waiting.

Q: **How many planes were in the first wave?**
a. 183
b. 202
c. 354
A: One hundred and eighty-three: 49 bombers, 51 dive bombers, 40 torpedo bombers, and 43 fighters.

Q: **What were the first planes to take off from the Japanese carriers?**
    a. High-level bombers
    b. Dive bombers
    c. Torpedo bombers
    d. Fighters
A: The fighters lifted off at approximately 0600, followed by high-level bombers, dive bombers, and finally the torpedo planes.

Japanese planes taking off before an ecstatic group of well-wishers. National Archives

Q: How long did the launching of the first wave take?
a. Fifteen minutes
b. Thirty minutes
c. Forty-five minutes
A: It took fifteen minutes to get all the aircraft airborne. Only one fighter was lost; it ditched in the ocean.

Torpedo planes taking off bound for Pearl Harbor. National Archives

Q: At what time did the planes head toward Pearl Harbor?
   a. 0615
   b. 0630
   c. 0645
A: The planes set their course at 0615.

Q: Who commanded the first wave?
   a. Commander Mitsuo Fuchida
   b. Lieutenant Commander Shigeharu Murata
   c. Lieutenant Commander Kakuichi Takahashi
   d. Lieutenant Commander Shigeru Itaya
A: Murata commanded the torpedo bombers, Takahashi commanded the dive bombers, and Itaya commanded the fighters. Fuchida had been designated the commander of the air fleet since September and, once airborne, had command over the operation.

Commander Mitsuo Fuchida, Flight Leader
of the Attack Force on Pearl Harbor.
National Archives

Q: When Commander Fuchida led his high-level bomber group across the *Akagi's* bow, what was he signaling?
A: That the flight formation was to set its course for Oahu. Fuchida had orders to drop the first bomb on Pearl Harbor as close to 0330 Tokyo time as possible. This would have timed the initial aggressive act within one-half-hour of Japan's notification to Washington that diplomatic relations were being cut.

Q: The sun rose as the pilots were flying toward Pearl Harbor. Of what did it remind them?
A: The 0626 sunrise shafts of light reminded many of the pilots of the Japanese Naval Flag. They considered this a good omen.

Q: At 0630 Admiral Nagumo launched sixteen floatplanes. What was their mission?
A: To search the areas east, west and south of the Task Force for any American ships and aircraft.

Q: At what time did the battle for Pearl Harbor actually begin?
    a. 0530
    b. 0645
    c. 0755
A: The battle began at 0645, when the USS *Ward* fired a shot at the midget submarine off the entrance of Pearl Harbor.

Q: How did the opening of the attack begin?
A: Dive bombers from the carrier *Shokaku* began the attack by blasting the seaplane base at Ford Island.

Q: When did KGMB radio station play music all night?
    a. When most of the military personnel were on pass
    b. When aircraft were coming in
    c. Weekend entertainment
A: The station provided a homing device for aircraft flying into Hawaii, including Japanese planes coming in on December 7.

Q: How did radio direction-finders work?
A: Pilots could find the exact direction a broadcast was coming from by turning the antenna.

Q: What did all the pilots from Japan have in common?
    a. All were between the ages of 22-30
    b. All were graduates of Eta Jima
    c. None wore parachutes
A: None of the Japanese pilots wore parachutes.

Q: What was the first ship to spot a Japanese submarine?
A: The supply ship USS *Antares*. It was waiting outside the harbor at 0630. The *Antares* saw what appeared to be a submarine conning tower. The *Antares* notified the USS *Ward*, which went to check. About this time, a PBY on routine morning patrol also saw the floundering submarine. Thinking that it was an American submarine in trouble, the pilot dropped two smoke pots nearby to help guide the *Ward*. At 0640, for the second time in less than three hours, the *Ward* sounded general quarters. Less than fifty yards away, and with all engines ahead full, the *Ward* commenced firing. The first round went high, but the second one found its mark at the water line near the base of the conning tower. The submarine then listed and apparently passed under the *Ward*. The *Ward* then released depth charges. A large oil spill formed on the surface and the submarine sank in 1200 feet of water.

Q: How did two Army privates give the Americans their last opportunity to go on the alert before the attack?
A: Roughly an hour before the attack on Pearl Harbor, two privates, Joseph L. Lockard and George E. Elliott, were at the mobile radar station near Kahuku Point. They began plotting a large sortie of aircraft. They called the Information Center at Fort Shafter and relayed the information to the controller on duty, Lieutenant Kermit Tyler, who was there only for familiarization. Believing that the flight was B-17's coming from the mainland, he told the two privates not to worry about it. A major error by the privates was

not stressing to the Lieutenant that the sighting contained more than 50 planes.

Q: **How did the Japanese plan to take advantage of the weather?**
A: High-level bombers would approach their targets against the wind to ensure the greatest success in bombing. Dive bombers would approach from downwind to maintain sharp angles of attack, plunge in steep and pull out low. Torpedo bombers were to come in close no matter what the weather conditions. After leaving the carriers, the torpedo bombers split into four groups northwest of Ewa. Two groups of eight planes each headed for the west side of Ford Island. Two groups of 12 planes each flew southeast then swung northwest in a large arc over Hickam and headed directly for Battleship Row.

Q: **What was used as the signal for the planes to get into attack formation?**
A: Commander Fuchida would indicate by a flare gun: one "black dragon" for surprise, two "black dragons" if surprise was lost.

Q: **At 0740, Commander Fuchida fired one "black dragon". What went wrong?**
A: After waiting 10-15 seconds, he thought that the fighters did not see the shot, so he fired another. The commander of the dive bombers mistook the second shot to signify surprise was lost. This meant the dive bombers would attack first, instead of the torpedo bombers.

Q: **Why did the first wave make its approach from the south?**
A: When Commander Fuchida heard KGMB radio station's weather broadcast for partly cloudy skies over Oahu and clouds mostly over the mountains, he decided the attack would have better conditions coming from the south, approaching Pearl Harbor from the ocean side.

Q: **How was the attack signal given to all the squadrons to form into a single column?**
A: The lead plane banked its wings sharply.

Q: **How many ships were in Pearl Harbor on December 7?**
    a.   84
    b.   96
    c.   145
A: There were 145 different types of vessels in Pearl Harbor on December 7, of which 96 were warships.

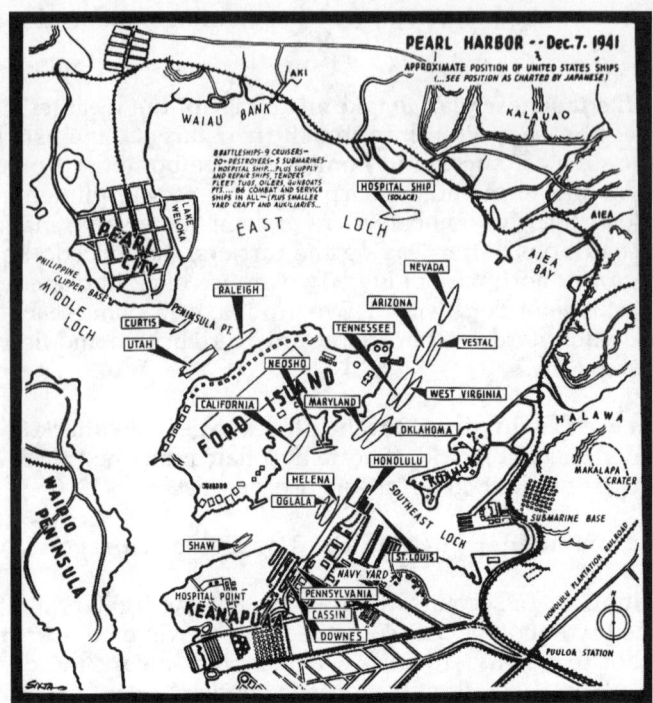

Location of the ships in Pearl Harbor on December 7. National Archives

Q: What type of American vessel was most numerous at the time of the attack?
A: Destroyers. There were 26 in Pearl Harbor that morning. The destroyers also put up the stiffest resistance during the attack.

Q: During the bomb runs, what was the distance separating the planes?
      a.   100 meters
      b.   200 meters
      c.   300 meters
A: Approximately two hundred meters.

Q: Who was responsible for giving the "go ahead" for dropping the bombs?
A: In the lead bomber, there were a specially trained pilot and a bombardier. At the lead plane's signal, the other planes released their bombs.

Q: How many bombs did each high level-bomber carry?
A: One 800-kilogram bomb, especially constructed from 16-inch naval shells and designed with delayed action fuses to penetrate the thick armor deck of the battleships.

Q: What was the mission for the Japanese fighters?
A: To help knock out the American airfields and intercept any Americans who might become airborne.

Q: At what time did the high-level bombers begin their attack?
A: At approximately 0805, 49 bombers, under direct command of Commander Fuchida, began their attack on Battleship Row.

Q: In December 1941, Japan had 10 aircraft carriers. The Americans had seven, three of which were in the Pacific. The Japanese were disappointed to find the American carriers gone. Where were they?
A: The USS *Enterprise* was headed back to Pearl after delivering planes to Wake Island, with an escort of nine destroyers and three heavy cruisers. The USS *Lexington,* with three heavy cruisers and five destroyers, was steaming toward Midway Island. The USS *Saratoga* was on the west coast, being overhauled and repaired.

Q: Why was it just luck that the USS *Enterprise* was not in the harbor?
A: The USS *Enterprise* was due in at 0730 that morning. When the attack was made she was still 150 miles southwest of Pearl Harbor because foul weather and refueling difficulties changed the *Enterprise's* arrival to the late morning or early afternoon.

Q: Why were so many ships in port?
A: With the carriers gone, the ships were vulnerable on the high seas without air cover. "War warnings" alerted the Hawaii commanders not to alarm the civilian population. Sudden departures of the bulk of the fleet on weekends would do just that. Also, the Navy could not keep more vessels at sea without seriously depleting fuel supplies.

Q: How many bombs did the Japanese dive bombers carry?
A: One 250-kilogram bomb.

Q: What were the Japanese planning to do if there were torpedo nets around the American ships?
A: If the ships were surrounded by nets, which would make the torpedoes ineffective, only the bombs would be used. Some of the torpedo pilots came up with the idea that they would dive into the nets to break the nets open.

Q: What did some squadron commanders tell their pilots to do if they developed engine problems and were unable to return to their carriers?
A: Officially, they were to try to make it to Niihau Island, which they thought was deserted, and from there be rescued by submarines. This order seems not to have been circulated throughout the assault formations. Some of the commanders stressed that they should crash into the nearest American ship or land installation.

Q: When and where was the first bomb hit at Pearl Harbor Naval Station?
A: The first bomb was dropped at 0755. It hit the PBY ramp at Ford Island.

Opening moments of the attack. The geyser of water in the center is a torpedo that just hit the USS *Oklahoma*. National Archives

Q: When and where did the first torpedo hit?
A: At approximately 0755, a pair of torpedoes slammed into the light cruiser USS *Raleigh* and the target/gunnery training ship USS *Utah*.

Q: What was the size of the torpedo used by the Japanese?
A: It was a 15-foot 800-kilogram Model 2 torpedo, fueled by oxygen.

FACT: Lieutenant Fusata Iida, who commanded the first wave of fighter planes, constantly spoke to his men about what to do if they developed engine problems once the attack started. Iida vowed that he would crash dive into the nearest enemy target. During the attack on Kaneohe Naval Air station, Iida's plane was badly damaged and crashed on a road. His body was put in a galvanized garbage can, not out of disrespect, but because there was no more suitable facility on hand. He was given a dignified military funeral with Americans who died that day.

Q: How far above the water's surface were the torpedo planes when they dropped their load?
    a. 20 meters
    b. 40 meters
    c. 60 meters
A: Some of the planes flew as low as twenty meters.

Q: How long after the first Japanese bomb had fallen did it take for the Americans to counter-attack?
    a. Five minutes
    b. Ten minutes
    c. Fifteen minutes
A: The Americans returned fire less than five minutes after the attack started.

Q: The return fire at Pearl Harbor was coming from the ships. What prevented the army's anti-aircraft guns around Pearl Harbor from firing at the invaders?
A: All the anti-aircraft ammunition was locked up in warehouses several miles away. The ships' anti-aircraft fire was slow because most of the guns were unmanned and the ammunition was stored under lock-and-key in the ships' magazines. The problem was solved by breaking the locks.

Q: When word reached him of the attack, what was Admiral Yamamoto doing?
A: He was playing shogi with one of his staff officers.

Q: What did Honolulu residents hear on the radio during the early stages of the raid?
    a.   Weather forecasts
    b.   Church music
    c.   News reports
A: Church music.

Q: During the attack, for what information did Japan's naval leaders wait?
A: The outcome of the torpedo attack on Battleship Row.

Battleship Row under attack. National Archives

Q: Where did the Japanese concentrate their attack?
    a.   Schofield Barracks
    b.   Navy ships and the Hawaiian Air Force
    c.   Ground installations at Pearl Harbor
A: On the navy ships and Hawaiian Air Force.

Q: What happened the very second the battleship USS *Nevada*'s band struck up the "Star Spangled Banner" and the color guard began to raise the flag?
A: A torpedo bomber, climbing after dropping its torpedo at the USS *Arizona*, crossed the *Nevada*'s stern. The plane's rear gunner fired a burst of machine gun fire. He missed the men but ripped the flag as it slid along the pole. The bandsmen did not take cover until the last note was played.

Q: What ship claimed to have shot down the first Japanese plane?
    a. USS *Honolulu*
    b. USS *Hulbert*
    c. USS *Ward*
A: The seaplane tender USS *Hulbert* claimed to have shot down a torpedo bomber at 0758.

Q: At the exact moment of attack, what was Admiral Kimmel doing?
A: He was on the phone with Commander Vincent Murphy, the Fleet Duty Officer, still receiving word about the USS *Ward*'s earlier action with a submarine. On hearing the attack, Kimmel slammed the phone down and ran outside, just in time to watch the torpedo bombers bomb his ships.

Q: Where did the dive bombers direct most of their attention?
A: Using an attack method of nine planes in single file, they concentrated on the ships anchored in the Middle and East Lochs, and along Ford Island.

Q: What did most people think was happening during the opening stages of the attack?
A: They thought it was target practice and realistic maneuvers. Oahu had grown accustomed to the noise.

Q: In the opening moments of the attack, were the Japanese aircraft the only ones in the air?
A: No, two private planes were aloft that Sunday morning. One pilot was making his approach into Rogers Field, after an early morning joy ride, and the other was giving instructions to a student pilot over the north shore of Oahu. The plane over north shore was fired at by Japanese gunners, but managed to escape and land safely at Rogers Field.

Q: In what direction were the battleships facing at the time of attack?
A: The battleships were always moored facing south toward the harbor's entrance on the east side of Ford Island.

Q: What battleship was the first to sound general quarters?
    a. USS *Arizona*
    b. USS *California*
    c. USS *Oklahoma*
A: At 0755, just seconds before the torpedo attack began, the *California* sounded the alarm.

Q: What was the first American ship to fire upon the Japanese?
A: The navy yard signal tower reported that the first ship to fire was the USS *Helena*. The time was 0801.

Q: What did the first bomb to hit Kaneohe Naval Air Station destroy?
A: The first bomb claimed the air station's only fire truck, crippling the Air Station's fire-fighting effectiveness.

Q: Why didn't Kaneohe Naval Air Station have any anti-aircraft batteries?
A: The army controlled the batteries and took them away earlier in the week.

Q: How much damage was done at Kaneohe Naval Air Station?
A: Twenty-seven PBYs were destroyed, six were damaged.

Q: During the attack, how did a bugler at Schofield Barracks rouse his regiment?
A: By blowing "pay call". By 0817, the Japanese had finished their attack on Schofield. A number of people on the post thought it was an earthquake.

Q: Who was Major General Maxwell Murray and what order had he given which violated military regulations and yet turned out to be a blessing in disguise?
A: Murray was the commander of the 25th Infantry Division at Schofield Barracks, the Army's largest outpost. He violated military regulations by moving all small arms ammunition into the barracks, thus allowing men to fire back immediately, once the attack began. He had been afraid that, if there was an attack and a direct hit was made on the magazine area, the explosion would kill hundreds of men who were drawing ammunition.

Q: What was the problem with the anti-aircraft rounds being fired?
A: The rounds were falling short of their targets; none were exploding close to the high-level bombers which were flying at 10,000 feet. For several days before the attack the battleships were replacing their standard-weight projectiles with heavier than standard-weight projectiles, by instruction of the Bureau of Standards, in a trade of distance for a more powerful explosive charge.

Q: How many planes were parked wing-tip to wing-tip on the hangar apron at Wheeler Airfield?
    a.   140
    b.   150
    c.   160
A: One hundred and forty fighter aircraft. By direct order of Major General Frederick Martin, Commander of the Hawaiian Army Air Corps, the planes were out on the hangar apron, instead of in the 125 protective bunkers with ceilings 8-10 feet high. Martin thought that it would be easier to guard against sabotage by parking the planes in the open.

Q: What was Lieutenant Akira Sakamoto's mission for the 25 dive bombers he commanded from the carrier *Zuikaku*?
A: As soon as Commander Fuchida gave his deployment order, the dive

bombers were to dash to Wheeler and put the base out of action as promptly as possible to prevent United States fighters from taking off and intercepting the first wave.

Planes parked wing-tip to wing-tip on Wheeler's apron, exploding.
National Archives

Q: **How did the torpedo bombers attack?**
A: Two or three planes were to attack each ship in single file, at a distance of 200 meters.

Q: **Where were most of the torpedoes concentrated?**
        a. Ships at sea
        b. Ships underway in the harbor
        c. East of Ford Island
A: On the east side of Ford Island, at Battleship Row.

Japanese bomber's view of Battleship Row from 10,000 feet. The oil is from the USS *Oklahoma* and the USS *West Virginia*. National Archives

Q: What was destroyed at Ewa Field?
A: Attacked during the opening stages of the first wave by fighters, the Japanese destroyed, or put out of commission, all forty-seven of the marine aircraft at that field. The only flyable planes remaining were the those from the USS *Enterprise*, which landed between 0835 and 0900.

Q: How many B-17's arrived from the mainland just as the attack started?
    a.   6
    b.   12
    c.   24
A: Twelve, each with a crew of five, flew into the opening stages of the attack. The planes were being shuttled to the Philippines, with a short stopover in Hawaii. They approached Hickam at 0815 with their bomb sights and machine guns still in packing crates.

Q: What important part did the Kahuku Golf Course play on December 7?
A: It served as a runway for one of the B-17's just arriving from the mainland. Seven landed at Hickam, two at Haleiwa, and one each at Wheeler and Bellows. Of the twelve, one was destroyed and three others badly damaged.

Q: Besides the B-17s, what other Americans unknowingly flew into the battle?
A: Eighteen aircraft sent ahead of the USS *Enterprise* were caught unexpectedly in the attack. Four were shot down by *Zero* fighters and one fell to American anti-aircraft. The rest landed safely at airfields around the island.

Q: What battleship was the first on Battleship Row to "die"?
    a.   USS *Arizona*
    b.   USS *Nevada*
    c.   USS *Oklahoma*
A: The USS *Arizona*. At 0810, the *Arizona*, moored at Battleship Row, was out of action. The first ship to "die" in Pearl Harbor was the USS *Utah*. Moored on the opposite side of Ford Island, it was put out of action eight minutes before the *Arizona*.

Q: What was a major hazard aboard the USS *Oklahoma* as it began to list?
A: The huge 1,400 pound shells used for the big gun turrets broke loose and started rolling, crushing everything in their way.

Q: How long after the first torpedo struck did the USS *Oklahoma* roll over?
    a.   20 minutes
    b.   1 hour and 20 minutes
    c.   The next morning
A: The battleship "turned turtle" only 20 minutes after the first torpedo struck her. The *Oklahoma* was preparing for a major admiral fleet inspection, scheduled for December 8. Contrary to normal procedure, all the watertight compartments below the water line were open, including the protective blisters. Once the *Oklahoma* was hit, the water rushed in.

USS *Oklahoma*. National Archives

Q: When the USS *Oklahoma* rolled over, 415 of the 1,354 crew members were entombed inside. How many were rescued?
    a.   360
    b.   148
    c.   32

A: Thirty-two were saved. The bulkhead had to be cut open. Some of the men had to wait until Monday afternoon to be rescued. Rescuers had to switch from acetylene torches to pneumatic cutting equipment when rescuers found that the acetylene torches burned up the oxygen in the hull, suffocating the trapped men.

Q: What did Vice Admiral Nagumo consider the most threatening force that the Americans could launch against his carriers?
A: Hickam's twelve B-17's.

Q: The United States battleships were moored in pairs. Torpedoes damaged the battleships moored outboard. What did the most damage to the ships on the inboard side?
A: The high-level bombers.

Q: When did Admiral Kimmel reach Fleet Headquarters?
    a.   At approximately 0755
    b.   At approximately 0805
    c.   At approximately 0830
A: Admiral Kimmel was in his office at approximately 0805.

FACT: After a grueling 14-hour flight, the B-17s which were being ferried from the west coast found themselves 100 miles off course, due to an inexperienced, young navigator. The navigator thought Oahu was north and recommended the planes turn right. The pilot double-checked and directed a left turn, heading southwest. Had the planes turned right, the B-17s would have met the Japanese planes head-on.

A B-17 at Hickam. National Archives

Q: **At what time did the explosion in the forward magazine aboard the USS *Arizona* take place?**
    a.   0755
    b.   0800
    c.   0805

A: The explosion that destroyed the battleship occurred at approximately 0805.

The USS *Arizona* exploding. National Archives

Q: **How did the explosion on the USS *Arizona* save the repair ship USS *Vestal* which was moored alongside?**

A: The USS *Vestal* was hit twice about 0805. The vacuum resulting from the USS *Arizona*'s explosion put out the fires aboard the *Vestal*. Although someone gave the order to abandon the *Vestal*, Commander Cassin Young ordered the crew back to their stations. Young ordered the ship under way and moved it several hundred yards from its berth. As the ship began to settle, he ran it aground near Aiea landing. Cassin's efforts to save his men and ship won him the Medal of Honor.

Q: What did Admiral Kimmel do after watching his ships being bombed in Pearl Harbor?
A: He walked alone into his office. When he returned, he had removed his four-star shoulder boards (he had been temporarily promoted to four-star rank) and replaced them with his permanent rank, two-stars. He demoted himself.

Q: What was the first ship to get under way?
A: The ready duty destroyer USS *Monaghan*, which already had a head of steam at the beginning of the attack.

Q: What was the first warship to clear the harbor?
A: The destroyer USS *Helm*. It was already under way when the attack began. It escaped from the chaos in the harbor at 0817.

Q: How experienced were the officers on aboard the USS *Aylwin*?
A: When the *Aylwin* put to sea at 0828, there were only four officers aboard, all ensigns, and only two of whom were qualified to stand top watch. The total sea experience of the four was a little more than a year. They were all Naval Reserve Training graduates.

Q: To the amazement of the Japanese, the Americans reacted promptly. Shortly after the attack began, black and white bursts from the anti-aircraft guns filled the air. What were the white bursts?
A: In their eagerness to fight back, the Americans were firing everything they had, including training shells which exploded in a white burst, instead of the black burst of war shells.

Battleships blazing from a distance. National Archives

Q: **Who was the station commander of Ford Island?**
    a.   Colonel William Farthing
    b.   Captain James H. Shoemaker
    c.   Commander Harold Martin
A: Captain Shoemaker. Colonel Farthing was the commander of Hickam Field and Commander Martin was the commander of Kaneohe Naval Air Station.

Q: **What Japanese warplane inflicted the most damage to the battleships?**
    a.   High-level bombers
    b.   Dive bombers
    c.   Torpedo bombers
A: Torpedo bombers, except for the bomb which caused the explosion of the USS *Arizona*. No torpedoes were known to hit the *Arizona*.

High-level bombers over Hickam. National Archives

Q: **How many American submarines were in Pearl Harbor at the time of attack?**
    a.   Four
    b.   Sixteen
    c.   Twenty-one
A: Four: the *Narwhal, Dolphin, Cachelot* and *Tautog*. The subs were generally ignored by the Japanese; none of them was seriously damaged.

Q: **What saved the battleship USS *California* from capsizing?**
A: After being hit by two torpedoes and two bombs, a young ensign took the initiative and immediately directed counter-flooding, which saved the ship. Unfortunately, after taking such a beating, the ship sank at its berth three days later.

Q: A reason frequently given for the bombing of the ex-battleship USS *Utah* was that, with its main decks stripped and heavy timbers laid across its decks to help absorb the impact of practice bombings, the *Utah* looked like a carrier. Why is this a myth?

A: The Japanese knew the *Utah* was an old ship and did not want to waste their bombs or torpedoes on it. Even with planks covering its deck, the old battleship in no way reassembled an aircraft carrier from the air. Even Commander Fuchida was upset that it was attacked. The best explanation is that it was bombed by mistake by an over-eager pilot.

Q: Of all the ships in Pearl Harbor that morning, the USS *Arizona* was considered to have "the most spirit". What did this mean?

A: It meant that the ship rated high in athletics and gunnery. High marks in this area brought a lot of pride to the crew, especially the enlisted personnel.

Q: Who was the captain of the USS *Arizona*?
    a. Captain Mervyn Bennion
    b. Captain Franklin Van Valkenburg
    c. Captain J. W. Bunkley
    d. Captain. F. W. Scanland

A: Van Valkenburg skippered the *Arizona*; Bennion was captain of the USS *West Virginia*; Bunkley, the USS *California*; and Scanland was captain of the USS *Nevada*.

Q: The commander of the Fleet Battleship Division died aboard his Flagship, the USS *Arizona*. Who was he?
    a. Rear Admiral Claude C. Bloch
    b. Rear Admiral Milo F. Draemel
    c. Rear Admiral H. Fairfax Leary
    d. Rear Admiral Isaac C. Kidd

A: Bloch was Commandant of Fourteenth Naval District at Pearl Harbor. Draemel was Commander of Destroyers, Battle Fleet. Leary was Commander of Cruisers, Battle Fleet. Kidd, the Fleet Battleship Commander, died aboard the *Arizona* during the attack, along with the *Arizona*'s captain, Van Valkenburg. Both men were posthumously awarded Medals of Honor for courageously discharging their duties in the face of the devastating attack.

Q: How much ammunition was stored in the USS *Arizona*'s magazines?

A: The *Arizona* stored almost 5,000 cans of powder, as well as over 100,000 rounds of machine gun and small arms ammunition. It also carried approximately 300 14-inch projectiles and 3,500 5-inch rounds.

Q: Whom did the Japanese credit with the incredible hit that destroyed the USS *Arizona*?

A: Petty Officer Noboru Kanai, one of the best bombardiers in the Imperial Fleet, from the carrier *Soryu*.

Q: At what time did the USS *Arizona*'s guns cease firing?

A: At about 0810, the guns stopped. Even though the *Arizona* had been hit, it had sounded general quarters, and its crew was shooting the anti-aircraft guns before it went down. At 0820, the senior officer on board, Lieutenant

Commander Samuel Fuqua, ordered, "Abandon Ship". Fuqua had tried valiantly to save his men and ship and ordered it abandoned only after the fires were out of control. He was the last man to step off the *Arizona*. For his intrepid actions and for saving numerous lives, he was awarded the Medal of Honor.

Q: How many of the *Arizona*'s crew were lost?
A: Of the 1,553 men aboard, only 289 survived.

FACT: The USS *Arizona* was hit by eight bombs. Some claim that the bomb that exploded the *Arizona* went down the smoke stack leading to the boiler room. The smoke stack was shaped like an inverted Y. A bomb dropped down the stack would have exploded in the boiler room. This would not have caused the terrible explosion. The wreckage showed the ship experienced a massive explosion in its forward part, the forward magazine. It was later discovered that the screens covering the funnels of the stack had not been penetrated.

The USS *Arizona* blazing. The USS *West Virginia* and USS *Tennessee* are in the background. National Archives

Q: Why was there no water pressure on Ford Island during the attack?
A: The *Arizona* had sunk on the 6" main water line. Firefighters had to use the water from a nearby swimming pool for their extinguishers.

Q: What was a major hazard in Pearl Harbor during the attack?
        a. Exploding ammunition stored in ships
        b. Burning oil on the water's surface
        c. Misdirected fire from ships
A: Burning oil, spreading across the water.

Oil burning on the water. The USS *Maryland* and USS *Oklahoma* are in the background. National Archives

Q: Was Schofield Barracks ever attacked?
A: There was no formal attack on the army post but, because it is across the road from Wheeler, some the planes attacking Wheeler over-shot their target and lightly strafed Schofield.

Q: What did Colonel Eugene Walker, Commander of Fort Kamehameha, do to camouflage his post?
A: In an effort to camouflage Fort Kamehameha, he ordered trucks to be driven back and forth in the loose soil to stir up as much dust as possible, thus creating a dust storm.

Q: What was important about Fort Kamehameha?
A: It was located adjacent to Hickam, on the east side of the channel that led to Pearl Harbor. Fort Kamehameha and Fort Weaver, which was located on the west side of the channel, were coastal satellites responsible for protecting the harbor from sea attack. There was a contingent of 2,500 men stationed at Fort Kamehameha. Japanese planes briefly strafed the area at 0813.

Q: How was Wheeler Field attacked?
A: At 0802, twenty-five dive bombers began their attack on Wheeler from the northeast. Flying in a "V" formation, they headed for the hangar line. Wheeler Field had no anti-aircraft guns, air raid shelters or trenches. The post had five machine guns mounted on a hangar and barracks. The planes had no ammunition on board. The ammunition was locked in the hangar. The first attack was over at about 0820. Seven Japanese planes in the second wave attacked at 0900. It lasted five minutes. Wheeler was targeted to knock out its fighter planes so they couldn't protect Pearl Harbor.

Wheeler Airfield on fire. National Archives

Q: **When did Bellows Field receive its first warning of a pending attack?**
A: Bellows, which is situated some eight miles southeast of Kaneohe, was strafed a little after 0830 by a lone *Zero* which made one run on the airfield and then flew off. No alarm was sounded. Bellows was not authorized ammunition. The men of the newly activated 298th Infantry, Hawaiian National Guard, who were camped nearby, had to go to ammunition tunnels at Diamond Head to secure ammunition.

Q: **Of all the battleships, the USS *Maryland* escaped with the least amount of damage. Why?**
A: In-board of the USS *Oklahoma*, it was protected from torpedoes. The *Maryland* did take two bombs from the dive bombers.

USS *Oklahoma* and USS *Maryland*. National Archives

Q: What was the greatest danger along Battleship Row?
A: It was not the Japanese bombs, but the tanker *Neosho*. The ship was docked at Ford Island's gasoline dock and, although it had unloaded its aviation fuel, it was full of high octane gas and was still attached to the gasoline dock with hoses. At 0842, the ship began to back away toward Merry Point. Fortunately, it was not damaged in the short trip across the channel.

Q: What did the *Neosho* do to help prevent its exploding from the scorching heat?
A: It had an internal steam-smothering system and smothered the gasoline fumes so they would not ignite.

Q: What accounted for much of the damage to the USS *Tennessee*?
A: Debris from the exploding USS *Arizona* caused more damage to the ship than the two bombs which hit it.

Q: How was the captain of the USS *West Virginia* killed?
A: Captain Bennion, severely wounded by a bomb fragment from the exploding USS *Tennessee*, directed his ship in battle until he died at his battle station. For his tenacious actions, he was awarded the Medal of Honor.

Q: A 22 year old Mess Attendant became the first black man to be awarded the Navy Cross. Who was he?
A: MA2 Doris Miller. Although he was a cook, and not trained in weapons, he grabbed a machine gun in the conning tower of the USS *West Virginia* and opened fire. Miller was also the *West Virginia*'s heavyweight boxing champion.

Q: How did some of the survivors escape the burning inferno aboard the USS *West Virginia*?
A: Using a five-inch gun as a bridge, they crossed over to the USS *Tennessee*.

USS *West Virginia* and USS *Tennessee*. National Archives

Q: How was the USS *West Virginia* saved from "turning turtle"?
A: By counter-flooding the ship slowly, it swung back to starboard and settled into the mud on an even keel. Men were trapped in the ship. Sixty-seven bodies were found in the hulk of the ship. Marks on a calendar showed that some lived until December 23, surviving on the trapped air and canned food.

Q: Where did the majority of the men from the abandoned and sunken ships finally end up?
    a. Ford Island
    b. 1010 dock
    c. Aboard the USS *Nevada*
A: Ford Island. It was the logical place for the surviving members of the ships moored along its shore.

Q: What was the Pearl Harbor Fleet Base Force Band's job in case of conflict?
    a. Man anti-aircraft batteries
    b. Carry ammunition
    c. Stretcher bearers
A: Stretcher bearers.

Q: How many bombs were dropped on Ford Island?
    a. 6
    b. 11
    c. 24
A: At least six exploded on or near the hangars. An estimated nine dive bombers took part in the attack on Ford Island's hangars and aircraft.

The destruction of Ford Island. National Archives

Q: The midget submarines had a specific mission during the attack. How did the Japanese refer to that mission?
A: They called it "Target A."

Q: At what time was a midget submarine spotted in the harbor?
   a. 0645
   b. 0758
   c. 0839
A: 0839.

Q: How many of the midget subs actually made it into Pearl Harbor?
A: Only one sub is definitely known to have entered the harbor, and it was sunk by the destroyer USS *Monaghan*. It is uncertain when the sub entered Pearl Harbor since the net had been opened at 0458 for the USS *Condor* and the USS *Crossbill*, and was not closed until 0840.

Q: How much damage was inflicted by the midget submarines?
A: None. The one that penetrated the harbor managed to fire its torpedo at the pursuing USS *Monaghan*, but missed.

Q: How long did the first wave last?
   a. 36 minutes
   b. 42 minutes
   c. 65 minutes
A: It started at 0753 and lasted approximately 42 minutes.

Q: Once the high-level bombers' bombing runs were completed, what were they to do?
A: Head for the rendezvous area to the west of Oahu.

Q: During the "lull", that period of time between the end of the first wave attack and the beginning of the second, where was much of the activity centered?
A: At 1010 dock. Many of the men, including some of the wounded, managed to swim ashore.

Q: What were Japan's aircraft losses during the first wave?
   a. 3
   b. 6
   c. 9
A: Three fighters, one dive bomber and five torpedo planes.

Japanese dive bomber falls to American anti-aircraft.
Hawaii State Archives

Q: Why did the garbage scow *YG-17* receive a commendation for its actions on the morning of December 7?
A: The scow sprayed down the USS *West Virginia* until the fire on the battleship was under control.

Q: How did the battleship USS *Tennessee* keep the flaming oil on the surface of the water away from the ship?
A: Fearing that the heat from the fire would ignite the ammunition, some of the magazines were flooded and the ship's screws were turned to keep the fire away from the ship.

Q: The Japanese did not know it, but one lucky hit at the Honolulu Harbor could have almost knocked Honolulu off the map. How?
A: There were 3,000 cases of dynamite at Pier 31A being unloaded from a cargo ship. The dynamite was to be used to blast runways from the coral atolls in the South Pacific.

Q: The army had a forward echelon, in case of attack. Where was it?
    a. Aliamanu Crater
    b. Diamond Head Crater
    c. Kolekole Pass
A: Aliamanu Crater, in old ammunition tunnels.

Q: At what time did Lieutenant General Short leave Fort Shafter to go to the Command Post?
A: About 0840, leaving only his chief of staff, Colonel Walter Phillips, with instructions to call General Marshall. The call was made at around 0900.

FACT: At 0839, the destroyer USS *Monaghan* received a signal from the seaplane tender USS *Curtiss* that a submarine was in the harbor. At 0840, the *Curtiss* opened fire and a shot passed into the conning tower, killing the sub's captain. The sub fired two shots, one at the *Curtiss* and one at the *Monaghan*; both missed. The *Monaghan* rammed the sub, sucking it under the destroyer. At 0843 the *Monaghan* dropped two depth charges, but the water was so shallow, the explosion damaged the *Monaghan*'s stern.

Q: What time was Alert 3 "full alert" announced by the army?
    a. 0815
    b. 0850
    c. 0900
A: At 0850.

Q: Why was the USS *Nevada* under way in only 45 minutes when it normally took at least two and one-half hours to build up enough steam?
A: Ensign Joseph Taussig, on duty that morning, ordered a second boiler lighted, to relieve the first boiler which provided power to the ship. He did this at 0840, just moments before the second wave attack began. The ship got underway at 0850.

Q: What hindered the USS *Honolulu* and the USS *New Orleans* from action during the attack?

A: In the excitement, the crews chopped away the power lines to the dock, leaving the ships with no power.

Q: What was the conduct of the men returning from shore leave?
A: Admiral Kimmel had one of his staff officers check on the men returning to base. His officer reported that the men were surprised and apprehensive about the attack but also eager to return to their ships to join the fight.

Q: How long after the first wave did the second wave of planes launch from the carriers?
    a. One-half hour
    b. One hour
    c. One and one-half hours
A: Roughly an hour after the first wave had cleared the carrier decks. They deployed at 0850 ten miles east of Kahuku Point.

Q: Who led the second wave?
    a. Lieutenant Commander Takashige Egusa
    b. Lieutenant Commander Shigekazu Shimazaki
    c. Lieutenant Saburo Shindo
A: The overall commander of the second wave was Lieutenant Commander Shimazaki, who was also in direct charge of the high-level bombers. Lieutenant Commander Egusa led the dive bombers and Lieutenant Shindo led the second wave fighters.

Q: Why didn't the Japanese include torpedo bombers in the second wave?
A: The Japanese decided that once the Americans were alerted, the anti-aircraft and the waiting United States fighter planes made it too dangerous. Also, smoke from the first attack would make it almost impossible for these slow-moving planes to make a clear sighting.

Q: Were there any crashes on the carriers during the take-off of the second wave?
A: No, but one of the dive bombers had to be pulled off because of engine trouble.

Q: At what time did the second wave attack begin?
    a. 0832
    b. 0854
    c. 0915
A: At 0854, almost an hour after the first wave.

Q: How many planes were in the second wave?
    a. 128
    b. 152
    c. 171
A: One hundred and seventy-one.

Q: How close to Oahu did the Japanese Task Force come?
    a. 100 miles
    b. 160 miles

      c.   180 miles
A: During the attack they moved to about 180 miles from the northern tip of Oahu. Knowing that many planes may be damaged, they wanted to be as close as possible to help in the recovery.

Q: What did the second wave choose as their targets?
A: Ships which were putting up the stiffest repelling fire and ships that suffered least from the first wave.

Q: Why was the second wave hit harder?
A: By the time the second wave arrived, the sky was covered with smoke and clouds. American ship and ground anti-aircraft batteries were waiting and ready.

Heavy anti-aircraft barrage greets the second wave. Hawaii State Archives

Q: What commanded the admiration and respect of the Japanese pilots?
A: "American Samurai", those pilots who managed to take off and who, despite being greatly outnumbered, flew straight in to engage.

Q: Who was America's first ally?
A: Holland. The Dutch liner *Jagersfontein*, inbound from the west coast, was at the entrance of Honolulu Harbor when bombs started falling around it at 0900. Since Holland was already at war, the ship was armed. Peeling the canvas cover from the guns, the crew began firing, the first of the Allies to join the fight.

Q: When was the first plane shot down in the second attack?
A: At 0905. It crashed near the USS *Curtiss;* several ships claimed the credit. At 0905, a disabled plane crashed into the *Curtiss* seaplane crane, possibly the war's first "Kamikaze." Twenty died and 58 were wounded.

Q: When and where did the USS *Nevada* run aground?
A: At 0910 at Hospital Point. The crippled *Nevada* was trying to escape the harbor when Japanese planes concentrated their attack on it. Afraid that if the ship sank, it would block the harbor entrance, Admiral Pye ordered it beached five minutes after its skipper, Captain Scanlan, came aboard. The *Nevada* had three officers and 47 enlisted killed, and five officers and 104 enlisted wounded.

Q: The USS *Montgomery* attempted an act of mercy for a downed Japanese pilot. What happened?
A: At 0930, a plane crashed into Middle Loch, 500 yards off the destroyer-minelayer. The USS *Montgomery* sent a boat to rescue the pilot and take him prisoner. The survivor resisted rescue efforts by pulling a gun. His "rescuers" had to shoot him.

Q: Who was the first Japanese prisoner of war?
A: Ensign Kazuo Sakamaki, who was captured on December 8, 1941. Sakamaki's disabled midget submarine floundered on the reef in Waimanalo Bay, off Bellows Field. Sakamaki and his fellow crew member Seaman Inagaki, abandoned the sub. Inagaki drowned in the surf. Sakamaki made it to shore and was captured by Sergeant David Akui of the 298th Infantry.

Q: When and where did the USS Shaw explode?
A: At approximately 0930, during the second wave attack. The *Shaw* was in Floating Drydock Two with the tug *Sotoyomo* and received three hits. Five bombs hit the floating drydock. Uncontrolled fires ignited the *Shaw*'s forward magazine. The explosion severed the ship's bow.

The explosion of ammunition magazines on the USS *Shaw*. National Archives

Q: At what time did the last Japanese plane leave the battle area?
   a. Approximately 0930
   b. Approximately 0945
   c. Approximately 1000
A: Just after 0930.

Q: **When did the USS *Oglala* order "abandon ship?"**
A: About 1000, the USS *Oglala* began rolling over just as Admiral Furlong stepped off the ship.

Q: **The skipper of the USS *California* gave orders to abandon ship at 1002. Why were men still aboard at 1030?**
A: The wind changed and blew the burning oil away from the ship by 1015. Captain Bunkley tried to get everyone on board again to fight the fires.

USS *California*. National Archives

FACT: As the attack began at Wheeler Field, Lieutenants George Welch and Kenneth Taylor jumped in their car and headed toward Haleiwa, where their squadron was temporarily training. They took off from the dirt field at Haleiwa in their P-40 fighters, shortly after the first wave attack was over. They headed toward Barbers Point and slid in behind a dozen Japanese planes just finishing their assault on Ewa Field. On their first encounter, they each shot down two planes. They continued in the fight until they needed more fuel and ammunition and headed back to Wheeler to load up on both. They took to the air again at 0900. A short time later, Taylor was wounded in his left arm and leg. After exhausting their ammunition, they returned to Wheeler. Taylor and Welch were given credit for shooting down a total of seven Japanese planes.

A Zero, trailing smoke, falls victim to anti-aircraft fire. Hawaii State Archives

Q: Wounded were coming into the dispensary at Pearl Harbor so fast, there wasn't much time for intensive treatment. What did the doctors and medics do?
A: Most of the wounded were given morphine to kill the pain. To make sure, the drug was not given twice, doctors marked an "M" on the patients foreheads with mercurochrome. The nurses aboard the hospital ship USS *Solace*, which was moored in the harbor, did the same thing, except they used lipstick.

Q: What drug did doctors credit with saving countless burn victims' lives?
A: Sulfa, which stopped the spread of infection.

Q: Did the Japanese Consulate in Honolulu know what was going on?
A: No, like most of the other residents, they thought maneuvers were going on.

Q: Which battleships received the most attention during the second attack?
A: The USS *Nevada*, USS *California* and USS *Pennsylvania*.

Q: What could possibly have been lucky about the two bombs that hit the USS *West Virginia*?
A: Both were duds and did not explode.

Q: What was Admiral Kimmel's flagship?
        a. USS *Nevada*
        b. USS *Pennsylvania*
        c. USS *Oklahoma*

A: The USS *Pennsylvania*. It was also the Pacific Fleet's Flagship. The USS *Pennsylvania* was normally docked at Dock 1010. Dive bombers attacked it at 0907, while it was in Drydock 1. Sixteen men died on the USS *Pennsylvania*.

The USS *Pennsylvania*, with the destroyers USS *Downes* and USS *Cassin*. National Archives

Q: Where was the Pacific Fleet Headquarters located?
    a. Ford Island
    b. Pearl Harbor Shipyard
    c. Pearl Harbor Submarine Base
A: Pearl Harbor Submarine Base.

Q: What was the damage to Bellows Field?
    a. Five planes
    b. Heavy damage to ground installation
    c. Complete destruction of planes and airstrip
A: Five planes.

Q: What were the losses to the second wave?
A: Six fighters and fourteen dive bombers.

Q: How long was it before the residents of Honolulu realized they were under attack?
A: For at least an hour after the attack began, most residents thought maneuvers were going on and were not aware that an actual attack was taking place.

Q: Why didn't the residents of Honolulu receive their December 7 morning newspaper?
    a. The newspaper building was sabotaged
    b. The presses broke down
    c. Newspaper employees were on strike

A: The *Advertiser*'s presses broke down after printing only 2,000 copies. Those went to the ships at Pearl Harbor. The rest of the island residents simply had to wait.

Q: What was done with the women and children housed at Fort Shafter immediately after the attack?
A: Nearly 400 residents were bussed to a large cave outside of Fort Shafter that was being constructed to be the new headquarters for the Coast Defense.

Q: Was the naval magazine at Lualualei ever bombed?
A: No. The magazine stored thousands of 14- and 16-inch projectiles. Each projectile was stored with two bags of between 75 and 90 pounds of smokeless powder. When questioned later why Lualualei was not targeted, Commander Genda replied that no one thought of it in the planning of the air attack.

Q: What were the losses to the USS *West Virginia*?
    a. 20 of 90 men
    b. 105 of 1,500 men
    c. 460 of 2,000 men

A: A young ensign on the *West Virginia* unknowingly saved hundreds of lives. When he heard an explosion and saw smoke and fire coming from near Ford Island, Ensign Roland Brooks thought the USS *California*, which was moored close to that area, was on fire. He ordered "away fire and rescue parties." Hundreds of men rushed topside, a move which saved many lives. Only one hundred and five of fifteen hundred men were lost.

Q: What were the losses to the USS *Nevada*?
    a. 25 men
    b. 37 men
    c. 50 men

A: Fifty men.

Q: What was a major source of confusion?
A: The radio stations, which broadcasted many rumors.

Q: What did "Beauty" Martin do to get his sailors ready after the attack?
A: The commander of Kaneohe Naval Air Station had his sailors bring their "whites" (white uniforms) to the mess hall and dipped them into pots filled with hot coffee to dye them brown.

Q: Why were Hickam's baseball field and post exchange bombed?
A: The Japanese map of the area was made in 1933. It was out-dated and inaccurate. The number of hangars was wrong (eight instead of five) and the baseball field was shown as a gasoline farm. The post exchange was identified as the headquarters building. The Japanese thought the facilities were cleverly camouflaged.

Q: What was the last major ship action in Pearl Harbor?
A: A sortie of the USS *St. Louis*. The USS *St. Louis* was known as the "Lucky Lou."

Q: How were the flames put out in the floating drydock?
A: In an attempt to prevent it from being destroyed, the drydock was flooded. Water and oil poured in. The burning oil ignited berthing destroyers' magazines and torpedo warheads, causing them to explode.

USS *St. Louis* steaming by the USS *California*. National Archives

Q: How many planes did the Hawaiian Army Air Corps have at the time of the attack?
        a.   About 200
        b.   227
        c.   425
A: Two hundred and twenty-seven.

AFTERWARD

Q: How were the fighters supposed to find their way back to the carriers?
A: They were not equipped with homing devices and the fighters were to rendezvous with the bombers.

Q: From which direction did the American Navy think the Task Force had come?
A: During the second wave attack, Hypo Station got a direction-finder bearing on radio signals made by the Japanese Task Force. The findings were bilateral, showing a reading of 003 or 183, making it either due north or south. Vice Admiral Halsey, aboard the carrier USS *Enterprise*, was still about 150 miles southwest of Oahu. Admiral Kimmel ordered him to locate the enemy forces and he proceeded on a fruitless chase southward.

Q: Where was the rendezvous point for returning Japanese aircraft?
    a. 20 miles northwest of the western tip of Oahu
    b. Over the channel between Oahu and Molokai
    c. 5 miles north of Kahuku Point
A: The planes were to rendezvous twenty miles northwest of the western tip of Oahu. There they were to join with the bombers, which were to lead them back to the carriers.

Q: Where were the midget submarines supposed to rendezvous with their "mother" submarines after the attack?
    a. Seven miles southwest of the island of Lanai
    b. Ten miles south of Diamond Head
    c. Five miles east of the island of Kauai
A: Seven miles southwest from Lanai. On the night of the attack, the "mother" submarines waited for the midget subs to return. None returned.

Q: What had the Honolulu Japanese Consul General, Nagao Kita, planned to do the morning of December 7?
A: He and his deputy, Otojiro Okuda, were scheduled to go golfing.

Q: What security measures did the Federal Bureau of Investigation (FBI) take following the attack?
A: At 1000 on December 7, Robert Shivers, the head of the FBI office in Honolulu, directed the Honolulu Police Chief to put a guard around the Japanese Consulate.

Q: What did Schofield Barracks soldiers do immediately after the attack?
A: They moved to defensive positions around the island. Everyone thought Hawaii was going to be invaded.

Q: A little after 1130, Governor Joseph Poindexter went on radio station KGU. What was his message?
A: He proclaimed a state of emergency.

Q: At what time were the public radio stations ordered off the air?
A: At 1142 radio stations were ordered by the military to remain off the air, except for special announcements. The military believed enemy planes might be using the radio signals as homing beacons.

Q: At what time did the Japanese Fleet leave the area?
A: At 1330 the Task Force headed back across the Northern Pacific.

Q: If Vice Admiral Nagumo had expanded his air reconnaissance around his Task Force, what would he have found?
A: He would have discovered the USS *Enterprise* while she was 150 miles southwest of Oahu.

Q: What information was retrieved from a downed Japanese plane?
A: A "plot board" and pilot's navigation sheet, found in the plane that crashed into the seaplane tender, USS *Curtiss,* showed a return route to the carriers and a temporary call sign card for all the ships that comprised the Task Force.

Q: What was the total loss of Japanese aircraft?
A: Twenty-nine were lost in battle. Sixty-one others were so badly shot up, they were beyond repair.

Q: How many Japanese carriers did the Americans believe had taken part in the attack?
A: Two.

Q: When did the Japanese Task Force break radio silence?
A: As the planes began to land back aboard the carriers, Vice Admiral Nagumo briefly broke radio silence and sent a short message to Admiral Yamamoto, summarizing the results of the attack.

Q: Once the planes arrived back aboard Vice Admiral Nagumo's flagship *Akagi*, what were the two things the Task Force Commander wanted to know?
A: First, had the American Fleet been damaged enough to put it out of operation for six months. Second, where were the carriers.

FACT: Two Seagull scout planes from the cruiser USS *Northhampton* flew into a Zeke at 1140, about 100 miles north of Kauai. After a 20-minute interchange, the Zeke flew off. No one really knew the Japanese carriers were north of Oahu until the Seagulls landed at Ford Island at 1527 and reported the attack.

Q: What was the reaction of the Japanese officers after the first attack wave returned to the carriers?
A: They were both excited and happy. The officers began to prepare for a second attack and were angered when Vice Admiral Nagumo ordered the Task Force to leave the area.

Q: How many Japanese ships were sunk on December 7?
   a. Six
   b. Fifteen
   c. None
A: None. However, four midget submarines were sunk.

Q: Why didn't Vice Admiral Nagumo launch a second attack against Oahu, despite the strong recommendations of Commanders Genda and Fuchida?
A: No one really knows, other than he lacked self-confidence in the operation and believed that Admiral Yamamoto was intent only on disabling the ships. Nagumo probably felt that he had accomplished his mission and that the shore facilities were not worth the risk. There was also the danger of the United States carriers returning to Oahu while the Japanese Fleet was in firing range. The Japanese then risked greater losses.

Q: How did not having a follow-up attack on the shore facilities affect the outcome of the war?
A: Since repair facilities were left intact, the United States was able to repair ships in record time, rather than have them go to the west coast.

Q: Was the cruiser USS *Portland*, which was escorting the USS *Enterprise* back to Pearl Harbor, bombed?
A: An excited American pilot, looking for the Imperial Fleet, thought the cruiser was part of the Japanese Task Force and almost bombed it.

FACT: Commander Genda prepared four plans to convince Vice Admiral Nagumo to conduct a second attack. All plans included a decision to stay about 200 miles north of Oahu to search and destroy ships not in Pearl Harbor, and/or to attack the naval base, ships and land facilities again. Each plan had a different route home: following the northern route; returning to Japan not as far north as was originally planned; following the Hawaiian chain to Midway; or sailing southward then west to the Marshall Islands.

Q: Why was Task Force One, commanded by Rear Admiral Milo Draemel, sent on a wild goose chase?
A: This makeshift task force was made up of the survivors of the Pearl Harbor attack. It included the light cruisers USS *Detroit*, USS *Phoenix* and USS *St. Louis*, along with a dozen destroyers. In the excitement of the attack, Admiral Kimmel ordered Draemel to search for the Japanese Task Force. When Admiral Kimmel realized Task Force One didn't have a chance against the Japanese Task Force, he ordered the task force to join with Vice Admiral Halsey.

Q: Once the public heard about the attack, blood donors began to appear almost immediately. This was fortunate, as the blood bank rapidly exhausted its supply of 200 bottles of blood plasma. The blood was taken so fast that one of the hospitals ran out of containers. What did it use to store blood in?
    a. Coca-cola bottles
    b. Giant pill bottles from the pharmacy
    c. Rubber gloves
A: Sterilized coca-cola bottles.

Q: When did Lieutenant General Short receive a copy of General Marshall's warning message?
    a. During the attack
    b. Nearly eight hours after the attack
    c. The next day
A: The message was handed to him nearly eight hours after the attack. He exploded. It arrived at the RCA Office in Honolulu at 0738 and was not marked "priority." It was given routine handling.

Q: How was the message delivered?
A: RCA messenger, Tadao Fuchikami, delivered it to the Adjutant General at 1145. It was decoded, then delivered to Lieutenant General Short at 1458.

Q: What happened to the "war warning" messages that were delivered to both Admiral Kimmel and Lieutenant General Short shortly after the attack?
A: They ended up in the trash cans.

Q: At approximately 1625 on December 7, Hawaii was placed under martial law and was subject to the rules of a military governor. Who was he?
A: Lieutenant General Walter C. Short. Short met Governor Poindexter in his office in Iolani Palace, shortly after noon at December 7, and briefed

Poindexter on the damages sustained. They discussed Short's fear of an invasion and uprising and Short asked that martial law be imposed. Poindexter reluctantly agreed only after calling President Roosevelt.

Q: After the attack, though damaged, how many of the battleships were still afloat and able to move under their own power?
    a. One
    b. Two
    c. Three
A: Three, the USS *Maryland*, USS *Pennsylvania* and the USS *Tennessee*.

Q: How many American aircraft were destroyed in the attack?
    a. 77
    b. 159
    c. 206
A: Ninety-four navy and 65 army planes were destroyed and many others damaged.

Q: In mid-afternoon, a B-17 from Hickam began a bomb run on what he believed was a Japanese carrier. Was it?
A: It was a carrier all right, except an American carrier, the USS *Enterprise*.

Q: It was estimated that one-third of the burn cases were fatal. Why did so many die from burns?
A: A majority of the cases were flash burns (third-degree) but they proved fatal because many of the men were not fully clothed, and much of their skin had been exposed. Within 24 hours after the attack, Tripler General Hospital had admitted almost a thousand casualties. Because the hospital was overcrowded, surgery (including amputations) was done in the hallways while the patients were lying in stretchers. The wounded were being taken to Tripler, Queen's Hospital, the Pearl Harbor Naval Hospital and several plantation dispensaries for treatment. All the medical facilities were overflowing with casualties.

Q: Why were guards posted at the Pearl Harbor morgue and on the abandoned battleships?
A: To prevent looting. Some of the sailors themselves were entering the morgue and the damaged ships looking for valuables.

FACT: For days after the attack, bodies were being pulled from the water and wreckage. Burial parties were kept busy. The Navy dead were buried at Oahu Cemetery and temporarily at Red Hill. Those buried at Red Hill were later reinterred at Punchbowl Cemetery. The Army buried their dead at the Schofield Barracks Cemetery.

Q: What important part did Honolulu's Major Disaster Council play immediately after the attack?
A: Organized in June 1941, it went into action as the attack started. Using every available means of transportation, it started an emergency ambulance service. The Council also sent much needed medical supplies to the military hospitals.

FACT: The *Tatuta Maru* left Japan on December 2, 1941, with a number of American and British passengers. The ship was bound for Los Angeles by way of Panama. Instead of following its published schedule, the *Tatsuta Maru* made a circle in the Pacific and returned to Japan on December 14. The American and British passengers were arrested and imprisoned when they disembarked from the ship. Those passengers were among America's earliest and most forgotten victims of Pearl Harbor.

Q: How many midget submarines were recovered?
A: Two. One was captured close to the southeast corner of Waimanalo Bay, near Bellows, when crew members failed to destroy it. The second one was sunk in Pearl Harbor by the USS *Monaghan*. It was recovered in late 1941 or early 1942.

Midget submarine. National Archives

Q: How many Japanese carriers did the Americans believe had taken part in the attack?
    a. Two
    b. Four
    c. Six
A: Two.

Q: Vice Admiral Nagumo expected a counterattack from the Americans. What plans did he make?
A: Once the planes returned to the carriers, the Task Force would begin immediate preparations to meet such a counter-attack. All dive bombers would convert to torpedo planes. If the counter-attack did not materialize, the tor-

pedo planes would be converted into high-level bombers.

Q: What proved to be Japan's most serious flaw in its attack on Pearl Harbor?
A: Vice Admiral Nagumo's decision to ignore the advice of Commanders Genda and Fuchida on making a follow-up attack and sending planes back to Pearl Harbor to destroy the oil storage and shore repair facilities. Also, had the Task Force remained in the area long enough to locate the American carriers the Japanese, with their superior force, could have possibly wiped out the American Fleet, thus forcing the Pacific Fleet to retire to the west coast. Japan needed to keep the Americans from interfering with their conquest of East Asia for at least six months.

Q: Did the Japanese ever really consider an invasion of Hawaii?
A: Admiral Yamamoto did seriously plan for an invasion and occupation of Hawaii. He felt that by doing so, the Japanese could use the islands as a bargaining chip to force the American government into a compromise peace. The Imperial Naval Staff briefly considered the idea, but rejected it, feeling that occupation of Hawaii was beyond Japan's capabilities.

Q: Where did Admiral Kimmel's staff believe the Japanese Task Force was located?
    a. North of Oahu
    b. West of Kauai
    c. South of Pearl Harbor
A: Most of Kimmel's staff believed that the Japanese were south. Some staff members believed that the Task Force had even encircled Oahu.

Q: What did Admiral Kimmel blame for the confusion during and just after the attack?
    a. Incompetent staff members
    b. "Fifth-columnist"
    c. False intelligence reports
A: Kimmel blamed "fifth-columnist" saboteurs for blocking his communication system by calling in numerous false reports. Kimmel was not alone in suspecting saboteurs. Army intelligence believed a large segment of the Japanese population was organized and prepared to attack military installations.

Q: At sundown, on December 7, what did everyone at Pearl Harbor hear?
A: Evening colors.

Q: What happened to the United States planes landing on Oahu on the evening of December 7?
A: Six fighters were coming in from the USS *Enterprise*. The pilots had trouble identifying their location because of the smoke and fire in the harbor, and flew past Oahu. Halfway over the Molokai Channel, they realized their error and turned around. On their approach to Pearl Harbor, American anti-aircraft guns began to fire at them. Two of the pilots died when their planes crashed. Two other pilots parachuted out, but one was killed before he landed. The remaining pilots landed with minor injuries.

Q: Why was so much attention given to Japanese sampan fishermen after the attack?
A: The United States Navy felt that the fishermen were really Japanese agents, giving vital information to the Japanese Fleet. Also, any Japanese raising pigeons were under suspicion because they might be "fifth-columnist" using pigeons for carrying messages to the Japanese Fleet off shore.

Q: Did Hawaii's Japanese population assist the Imperial Fleet in any way?
A: Intensive investigations after the attack uncovered no instance of collaboration between the Japanese Navy and Hawaii's American Japanese. There was one incident on Niihau (The Battle of Niihau) where a storekeeper of Japanese ancestry helped a downed Japanese pilot after the pilot crashed landed on Niihau.

Q: What happened during the Battle of Niihau and how did two civilians win commendations?
A: The Island of Niihau is privately owned by the Robinson family, who live on the Island of Kauai. The only residents were Hawaiians and two Japanese families who worked for the owners. During the attack on Pearl Harbor, one of the Japanese fighter planes, piloted by Shigenori Nishikaichi, crashed landed on Niihau. One of the Hawaiians, Howard Kaleohano, grabbed the pilot out of the plane, took his papers and had Nishikaichi confined. For several days, the residents tried to signal Kauai by building fire signals, but no one answered. In the meantime, the Hawaiians asked the Japanese living there to act as interpreters. After five days, Nishikaichi convinced one of the Japanese to help him escape. They locked the lone guard up, went to Kaleohano's house to retrieve Nishikaichi's papers, and burnt the house down. They then removed the machine guns from the disabled plane and took control of the village. Kaleohano and some of his friends rowed to Kauai that night to get help. Sixteen hours later they arrived on Kauai and reported the intruder. When the military officials arrived, they found that the residents had solved the problem. Nishikaichi had threatened two of the villagers, Benjamin Kanahele and his wife. During the ensuing fight, Kanahele was shot several times. He got so angry, he picked Nishikaichi up and threw him against a stone wall, killing him. Nishikaichi's accomplice was so frightened, he committed suicide. For their actions, Kaleohano was decorated with the Medal of Freedom. Kanahele was given the Medal of Merit and a Purple Heart.

Q: When the police entered the Japanese Consulate, what were the members doing?
A: Several Honolulu policemen entered the consulate. Finding one of the doors to an office locked, they kicked it in. In a bathtub which had been placed in the middle of the floor, consulate members were burning code books.

Q: What effect did martial law have on Hawaii?
A: All civil authorities were placed under military control. Censorship of mail, fuel control, blackouts, and curfew was enforced. Press censorship was also effected, which prohibited criticisms which would embarrass the military and which affected the licensing system for newspapers. It also appeared to

affect the legal system, with prosecutors, by 1942, having an extraordinary conviction rate of 98%.

Q: What was the reaction of the civilians on the outer islands in the days immediately following the attack?
A: They were a little fearful and very confused. Newspaper and radio censorship prevented them from getting accurate information. They really did not know what to expect next.

Q: How long did Hawaii remain under martial law?
A: Until October 1944.

Q: What was the "grab list" that the FBI kept?
    a. People to be arrested
    b. Codebooks to be confiscated
    c. Buildings to be occupied in emergency
A: Military intelligence prepared a list of people whom they believed would aid Japan's war effort. It included consular agents, Shinto priests, fishermen and community leaders.

Q: How many Japanese were arrested on December 7 and incarcerated?
    a. Approximately 400
    b. Approximately 1000
    c. Approximately 1400
A: Under martial law, persons could be arrested and detained without trial because the writ of habeas corpus was suspended. Within 24 hours, the FBI, police, and army and navy intelligence rounded up 300-400 of those listed on the "grab list". Although most were Japanese, some Italians and Germans were also arrested. Some fourteen hundred people were arrested and held at detention camps on Sand Island.

Q: Initially, the plan was mass internment of all of Hawaii's Japanese population. What stopped this from happening?
A: Hawaii's Japanese population was too large and too important a part of Hawaii's work force. Interning them would cripple the economy. Japanese farmers provided the majority of Hawaii's food supply. Even of the 1,400 arrested, only 1,000 were relocated to the continental United States.

Q: What did the government do to protect currency?
A: Imprint "Hawaii" on the bills. This made the currency useless outside Hawaii and, in case of invasion, it would be of no use to the enemy.

Q: Forty-four projectiles fell on the City of Honolulu causing some $500,000 in damages and numerous civilian casualties. How many bombs fell from Japanese planes on the city?
    a. 1
    b. 23
    c. 44
A: Hawaiian Department ordnance specialists who surveyed the impact sites revealed that all but one of the forty-four were improperly fused anti-aircraft rounds.

Q: What was the "Battle of the Tank Farm"?
A: There was a sizeable tank farm not far from the submarine base. For a couple of nights after the attack, Army sentries patrolled the perimeter and Marines patrolled the interior tank farm property. They ended up shooting at each other.

Q: What was the total of United States casualties?
A: Two thousand four hundred and three dead and 1,178 wounded. The explosion to the *Arizona* accounted for most of the navy and marine dead. The majority of army casualties were air corps personnel at Hickam and Wheeler. The majority of the civilian casualties were from falling anti-aircraft shells.

Q: When did the first ship load of casualties sail for the continental United States?
A: Christmas Day, December 25, 1941.

Q: What was the total Japanese loss of life for the Pearl Harbor attack?
    a. 27
    b. 64
    c. 129
A: Deaths from both waves combined were 55, and nine of the midget submarine crew also died, making a total loss of life of 64 on December 7.

Q: Who did Emperor Hirohito want to see when the Task Force returned?
A: Vice Admiral Nagumo, and Commanders Fuchida and Shimazaki.

Q: What was the total damage to American aircraft?
A: The navy's losses were eighty-seven planes of all types. The Hawaiian Air Force lost four B-17's, thirty-two P-40's, two A-20's and twenty-five other, mostly obsolete, planes. Also to be added among the losses were one of the B-17's that had just arrived from the mainland that morning, and the eleven planes from the carrier *Enterprise* which were shot down that morning by the Japanese and by United States anti-aircraft fire that evening. This made the total loss for American aircraft for December 7 at 162.

Q: How bad was the damage to American ships in Pearl Harbor on December 7?
A: Out of the eight battleships, five were sunk or severely damaged. The remaining three were temporarily out of service. The target ship USS *Utah* and the minelayer USS *Oglala* were capsized. Three light cruisers, USS *Raleigh*, USS *Honolulu* and USS *Helena*, were hard hit. The destroyers USS *Downes*, USS *Shaw*, USS *Cassin* and USS *Helm*, were crippled. Floating Drydock Two was practically destroyed and the repair ship USS *Vestal*, the tugboat *Sotoyomo* and the seaplane tender USS *Curtiss* were badly hit. Including the drydock and tugboat vessels sunk or damaged, the number comes to twenty-one.

Pearl Harbor in the afternoon of December 7. Hawaii State Archives

Q: What battleships were totally lost?
    a. Two
    b. Four
    c. Six
A: Miraculously, only two, the USS *Arizona* and USS *Oklahoma*.

Q: What ever became of the battleships that were at Pearl Harbor on the morning of December 7?
A: The USS *Pennsylvania*, USS *Maryland* and USS *Tennessee*, the most lightly damaged of all the battleships, were ready for action in less than two weeks after the attack. The USS *Nevada* was back in service before the end of 1942, the USS *California*, by the middle of 1943. The USS *West Virginia* was ready for action in the summer of 1944. Both the USS *Arizona* and the USS *Oklahoma* were too badly damaged to see service again.

Q: The USS *Arizona* was officially removed from the active list of commissioned ships on December 1, 1942. What happened to the USS *Oklahoma*?
A: Too badly damaged to be worth the expense of refitting, the *Oklahoma* was decommissioned in September 1944. It was sold for $46,000 scrap to a San Francisco salvage dealer. On May 17, 1947, it sank while being towed to the mainland.

Q: How did the United States Navy's losses compare to previous conflicts?
A: The Navy suffered three times the losses it incurred during the Spanish American War and World War I combined.

Q: How much of the battle force at Pearl Harbor was lost?
   a. One-half
   b. Three-quarters
   c. All
A: Three-quarters.

Q: What caused the biggest loss of life in Pearl Harbor?
A: The exploding of the USS *Arizona*.

Q: Exceptional acts of bravery were common on December 7th. How many men won the Medal of Honor?
A: Sixteen Medals of Honor were given; 11 were awarded posthumously.

Q: What were some of the common rumors after the attack?
A: Japanese laborers had cut arrows in the cane fields, the water was poisoned, Russians had bombed Tokyo, paratroopers were in Waikiki, San Francisco was under attack, and that the USS *Enterprise* Task Force had been destroyed.

Q: Who were the Japanese paratroopers landing at Ewa plain?
A: They turned out to be a group of Japanese sitting by the road side waiting for transportation, with white canvas bags holding their personal belongings. The plantation workers were being moved to different quarters.

Q: How did the United States miss its best chance of a pre-attack warning?
A: By not deciphering the message between the Honolulu Japanese Consulate and Tokyo fast enough. RCA turned over messages from Japan to military intelligence. Most were coded and dated December 3 and 4. It was December 10 before all were deciphered and translated. The messages showed Tokyo's anxiety to have information concerning conditions at Pearl Harbor. There was no reason Japan would need the information, unless they planned to use it against ships while the ships were in the harbor.

Q: The FBI knew that the entire espionage in Hawaii was centered around the Japanese Consulate. Why didn't the United States take action against them?
A: The consulate was protected by diplomatic immunity.

Q: Why did Secretary Hull receive Ambassador Nomura and special envoy Kurusu, when he knew that Pearl Harbor had already been attacked?
A: Secretary Hull received them at 1420 Eastern Standard Time, hoping one chance out of a hundred that the report of the attack was not true.

Q: Was the attack on the USS *Monaghan* the first attack by a Japanese submarine against an American ship?
A: No. The first sub attack was against the steam schooner *Cynthia Olsen*. The ship was half-way between Seattle and Honolulu when it radioed it was under attack by a submarine. No trace of the ship or its crew was ever found.

Q: What was Secretary of War Stimson's reaction to the news of the attack?
A: Relief that the indecision of joining the war was over. Stimson knew the Americans would rally once attacked.

Q: How quick was President Roosevelt's response to news of the attack?
A: Within three hours (1600 Eastern Standard Time), Stephen Early, the White House Press Secretary, announced that President Roosevelt was preparing his declaration of war.

Q: What was Proclamation 2525?
A: On December 7, President Roosevelt signed a proclamation granting authority to the Department of Justice to detain "enemy aliens".

Q: Why did the Americans consider the attack on Pearl Harbor a sneak attack?
A: Because no declaration of war had been made prior to the attack.

Q: Was it really a sneak attack?
A: Not to the Japanese. Within Japanese tradition, the samurai constantly used it. Anyone who did not take advantage of the first blow was considered a fool, while the man who undertook the preemptive strike was regarded as intelligent.

Q: Where else did the Japanese attack on December 7, other than Pearl Harbor?
A: Guam, Wake Island, Philippines, Singapore, and the British Colony at Hong Kong. At Shanghai, the Japanese captured the gunboat *Wake* and imprisoned her crew.

FACT: Japanese submarines practically laid siege to Hawaii in the weeks following the attack. Several ships were torpedoed and sunk in waters surrounding the Islands. Every now and then, a submarine would surface and fire a round or two at some ground installation, doing very little damage. It was probably done more to fray people's nerves than to do serious damage.

Q: What did the United States military authorities in Hawaii consider one of their first orders of business?
A: Evacuation of military dependents. Within a very short time after the attack more than 25,000 people had sailed for the mainland.

FACT: Almost immediately after the attack, civilian volunteer groups began organizing. The biggest group was the Organized Defense Volunteers. Under the control of the Army, it was a reserve force whose purpose was to perform guard duties and participate in riot control. Another very important group was WARDS (Women Air Raid Defense). Also under the Army's control, the WARDS' primary job was plotting planes.

Q: What hindered a successful diplomatic solution between Japan and America?
A: Neither side made frank presentations of their country's position. Both thought they were in close touch with the heads of their governments. The

proposals made by each ambassador caused great misunderstanding and increased suspicion on both sides.

Q: What happened to the American and Japanese Ambassadors after the attack?
A: American Ambassador Grew and the embassy staff were confined to the American Embassy in Tokyo. Ambassador Nomura and his embassy staff were sent to a hotel in Hot Springs, Virginia. It was the middle of June 1942 before each was allowed to return to his country.

Q: The Japanese had used the German Kuehn in their spy network in Honolulu. What finally became of him?
A: Kuehn was arrested and tried by military court and sentenced to death. His sentence was commuted to life imprisonment and he was shipped off to the mainland for confinement. When the war ended, he was returned to Germany and released there.

FACT: The Washington Post printed the following article: "The very fact that the United States Pacific Fleet was undermanned, inadequately supplied and generally unprepared for a slugging contest with the Japanese Navy...intensified the necessity for making every precaution against the sort of attack which the Japanese launched...The great mystery is why, with so much knowledge of what the Japs were doing, was there so little action."

Q: Did Japan make a second attack on Pearl Harbor?
A: Yes. on March 4, 1942. It was called Operation K. Japan was concerned about how fast the fleet was being repaired. Two new Kawanishi HED1 (Emily) flying boats were used because they could fly non-stop from Japan's base in the Marshall Islands. American radar detected the planes and four P-40s were sent to intercept them. Both planes missed Pearl Harbor and dropped their bombs without causing damage. Both bombs fell in the mountains behind Honolulu. The Japanese also launched a reconnaissance plane from a submarine off Oahu in October 1943. Its mission was to check on construction at Pearl Harbor and Hickam.

Q: How many inquiries/investigations were conducted about United States lack of preparedness at Pearl Harbor?
        a. 1
        b. 6
        c. 9
A: A total of nine.

Q: Who conducted the first inquiry on what happened at Pearl Harbor?
A: Secretary of the Navy Frank Knox. He flew to Hawaii, arriving on December 11. Secretary of War Stimson also sent army investigators, but their plane crashed on the West Coast.

Frank Knox, Secretary of the Navy. National Archives

Q: What was President Roosevelt's reaction to Secretary Knox's report?
A: Roosevelt was not happy. Knox reported that neither Admiral Kimmel nor Lieutenant General Short were derelict in their duties. Neither officer had access to the decoded Japanese messages and they were hindered by conditions beyond their control e.g. not enough planes and anti-aircraft guns.

Q: What significant changes in leadership occurred on December 16, 1941?
A: Secretary of War Stimson and Secretary of the Navy Knox relieved Lieutenant General Short and Admiral Kimmel of their commands. The reason given, "not on alert".

FACT: On December 16, Admiral Kimmel received a dispatch informing him that he was to relinquish command at 1500 hours the following day. Admiral Pye was then temporary Fleet Commander for 14 days until Admiral Chester Nimitz took permanent command. Lieutenant General Delos C. Emmons replaced Short on December 17 as Commander of the Hawaiian Department.

Q: How was responsibility for the surprise attack determined?
A: The Roberts Commission was convened to investigate allegations of negligence. It was headed by Justice Owen J. Roberts.

Q: Why wasn't disciplinary action taken against Admiral Kimmel and Lieutenant General Short right after the Roberts Commission Report was issued?
A: There was a general agreement that any disciplinary action would have to wait until after the war was over. However, congress did not forget and both individuals were asked to waive their rights to immunity because of the statute of limitations.

Q: General Douglas MacArthur had at least a six-hour warning that war had started. He still left his planes at Clark Field, in the Philippines, on the ground and open to attack. Most of them were destroyed by the Japanese. Why was no action taken against MacArthur when Lieutenant General Short was being relieved for "not on alert"? MacArthur was guilty of the same offense.
A: No one really knows. Perhaps it was his popularity with the American public and Washington officials or perhaps he was considered too valuable to lose.

Q: What happened to Admiral Kimmel and Lieutenant General Short's military careers after Pearl Harbor?
A: Both Short and Kimmel were "invited" to retire. Lieutenant General Short retired on February 28, 1942 while Admiral Kimmel retired March 1, 1942.

Q: After their retirements, how did both men contribute to the war effort?
A: Short joined the Ford Motor Company in Dallas, Texas. That plant manufactured only war materials. Kimmel joined Frederick R. Harris, a ship building firm. His knowledge helped the company solve a number of technical problems.

Q: How many military investigations were conducted?
    a.   1
    b.   3
    c.   5
A: The military conducted five. The Army Pearl Harbor Board conducted their investigations from July 20 to October 20 1944. The Navy Court of Inquiry was conducted July 24 through October 19, 1944. At the direction of the Secretary of the Navy, James Forrestal, Admiral Hewitt conducted another navy investigation. General Marshall, who was criticized by the Army Board, directed Colonel Carter Clark to conduct another army investigation. Secretary of War Stimson, also dissatisfied with the criticism of Marshall, directed Major Clausen to conduct another investigation.

Q: What personal tragedy happened to Admiral Kimmel in the midst of the investigation?
A: Kimmel's son, Lieutenant Commander Manning M. Kimmel, died on September 6, 1944, while commanding the submarine *Robalo*.

Q: What was a major obstacle to both investigative bodies?
A: The military was still keeping Magic, i.e. the code breaking interceptors, a secret.

Q: How did America's and Japan's misconceptions affect the war?
A: If there was any blame to be placed for Pearl Harbor, it was probably on the American views of the Japanese. Americans thought of Japan as a poor country populated by people who were good copiers with no creativity. There were sufficient warnings that Japan was getting ready for war. Americans failed to believe it. Even after the attack, there was some speculation that Germany had masterminded the plan.

Q: What unexpected event occurred because of the attack which Japan did not anticipate?
    a. They did not destroy the whole fleet
    b. The attack failed to sink the carriers
    c. The United States became infuriated
A: It not only infuriated the United States; it rallied Americans into a war they would not allow themselves to lose.

Q: Did Japan really knock-out the United States with its victory at Pearl Harbor?
A: No. The repair facilities were virtually untouched and in good shape. The sub-base was barely touched and carriers and destroyers and cruisers were available. If Japan had gone ahead with a southern move into Malaya, Thailand and the Philippines, Japan might have had a better chance of drawing the American Fleet into the western Pacific early.

Q: Why should Washington receive most of the blame for Pearl Harbor?
A: Two reasons. First, Washington put most of its concentration on the situation in Europe and underestimated the situation in the Pacific. Second, hardly anyone in the capital paid any attention to their field commanders, Admiral Kimmel and Lieutenant General Short, and what they thought of the situation.

Q: What did Admiral Chester Nimitz, the new Fleet Commander, think of the way the navy treated Kimmel after the attack?
A: Nimitz thought that Kimmel had not been given a "fair shake" and that he was being used as a scapegoat.

Q: When did Admiral Kimmel learn of the fourteen point message sent from Japan which was a clear indication that war was imminent?
A: During a hearing in February 1944.

FACT: Prime Minister Winston Churchill was able to read the Purple diplomatic messages as well as the JN-25 throughout the months leading up to Pearl Harbor. He may very well have known that the Task Force had left and could possibly be heading for Hawaii and kept this information from Roosevelt because he wanted the Americans in the war.

FACT: In retrospect, Admiral Nimitz was glad that Admiral Kimmel did not know that an attack was coming. Kimmel most surely would have gone out to meet the Japanese Fleet and a good many, if not all, of the United States ships would have been sunk because of Japan's superior air power. The way it worked out was bad enough, but at least most of the ships were repaired in an amazingly short period of time, since the repair facilities at Pearl Harbor were left untouched.

Q: What formal charges were brought against Admiral Kimmel and Lieutenant General Short?
A: Neither was ever formally charged with dereliction of duty or errors of judgement.

Q: What happened to Lieutenant General Short after the congressional inquiry?
A: By the end of the final inquiry into the attack on Pearl Harbor, Short was not in good health. He died quietly at his home in Dallas, Texas, on September 3, 1949, at age 69. Until his death he kept to himself his views about what happened at Pearl Harbor.

Q: What happened to Admiral Kimmel after the congressional inquiry?
A: He left the Frederick Harris Company in 1947 and moved to be near his son in Connecticut. Kimmel died on May 14, 1968 at the age of 86.

Q: How was Admiral Yamamoto killed?
A: American intelligence intercepted Yamamoto's itinerary for April 18, 1943. The admiral was making an inspection tour of his forward bases. Yamamoto was known to rigidly follow his time table and the Americans could predict his movements. A flight of American P-38s ambushed his flight and sent it in flames into the Bougainville jungle.

Q: How did to Vice Admiral Nagumo meet his end?
A: Nagumo committed suicide in June 1944, as the Americans were advancing on Saipan and the fall of the island was imminent.

Q: What happened to General Hideki Tojo, Prime Minister/Minister of War?
A: Toward the end of the war, Tojo fell out of favor. After the war ended, and during the occupation, he tried to commit suicide by shooting himself in the chest as the Americans came to arrest him at his home. He survived and was tried at the Tokyo War Trials. He was convicted of crimes against humanity and in 1948, he was hanged.

Q: What became of Ambassador Nomura?
A: After returning to Japan in the summer of 1942, he "retired", with no military or naval duties. Nomura died in 1964.

Q: What happened to the "little L shaped cow pasture" known as Rogers Field?
    a. It became Naval Air Station Barbers Point
    b. It's now the Honolulu International Airport
    c. It's now called Kapiolani Park
A: It became Honolulu International Airport.

Q: When was Japan convinced that the JN-25 code had been broken?
A: In September 1942, when captured Ultra material showed the detail movements of Japanese warships prior to the battle at Midway.

FACT: Admiral Kimmel's great dereliction was his failure to maintain the proper state of readiness. Kimmel's predecessor, Admiral Richardson, maintained 300-mile air patrols from Hawaii from May 1940 to December 5, 1940. Kimmel stopped the flights when Admiral Stark, Chief of Naval Operations, wrote that he didn't believe they were necessary "at this time." Had Admiral

Kimmel conducted the same reconnaissance, the Pearl Harbor disaster would not have occurred.

Q: How did the lessons learned from Pearl Harbor affect the structure of the United States government?
A: Congress created an intelligence agency specializing in foreign intelligence, the Central Intelligence Agency (CIA). It also brought all the military under a single agency, the Department of Defense.

Q: How did one scared nineteen year old company clerk, stationed at the 27th Infantry Regiment at Schofield Barracks, popularize the attack on Pearl Harbor?
A: Novelist James Jones, several years after the battle, forever etched the attack in the minds of Americans through his book, *From Here To Eternity*.

FACT: In June 1942, a special battalion made up of Americans of Japanese Ancestry (AJA) from Hawaii was formed, called the 100th Battalion. The recruiting station was flooded with thousands of American Japanese wanting to volunteer. The 100th Battalion was sent to train in Wisconsin and Mississippi, and then sent overseas in the Fall of 1943. There it saw heavy action in Italy, where heavy casualties were suffered. In 1944, the 100th Battalion was absorbed by the 442nd Regimental Combat Team, the "Go For Broke" outfit which was composed of AJAs from Hawaii and the continental United States. In September 1944, the 442nd was involved in further fighting in France, where it rescued what is now known as the "Lost Battalion", a unit from Texas which had been cut-off and surrounded for several days. The Texas legislature, to show its appreciation, made the members of the 442nd honorary citizens of their state. In the Spring of 1945, the 442nd was back in Italy, where it finished out the war. It was nicknamed "the Purple Heart Regiment". Over 2,000 Purple Hearts were awarded. The 442nd was the most decorated unit in World War II.

QUOTES

Q: Who said, "One day, Japan would go to war with the United States for supremacy in the Pacific"?
A: In October 1924, General Billy Mitchell made this prediction in a report to the United States War Department. He believed it would be a surprise dawn attack by carrier-based airplanes against Pearl Harbor and Schofield Barracks. Mitchell's report was filed away and ignored.

Q: Who wrote this memorandum: "Every Japanese citizen or non-citizen on the island of Oahu who meets Japanese ships or who has any connection with officers or men should be identified and listed for placement in a concentration camp in event of trouble"?
A: President Franklin Roosevelt, 10 August 1936.

Q: Who wrote, "It seems to me increasingly clear that we are bound to have a showdown some day, and the principle question at issue is whether it is to our advantage to have that showdown sooner or later"?
A: America's Ambassador to Japan, Joseph Grew, wrote this to President Roosevelt on December 14, 1940, because of his concern about Japan's expansionist policy.

Q: Who made this statement, "If there were ever men and a fleet ready for an emergency, it's Uncle Sam's fighting ships"?
A: This was printed in the *Honolulu Advertiser* on February 1, 1941.

Q: "The American commander is no ordinary or average man, such a relatively junior admiral would not have been given the important position of CINCUS unless he were able, gallant and brave." Who said it and to whom was he referring?
A: Admiral Isoroku Yamamoto referring to Admiral Husband Kimmel, who was a Rear Admiral (two grades lower) before being appointed as CINCUS.

Q: "Whether rightly or wrongly, the people of the United States seem to believe all the so-called experts' claims that Japan has only two bathtubs in the Navy, no money, no oil, and all Japanese fliers are so cross-eyed they couldn't hit Lake Michigan with a bomb." Where did this appear?
A: It was published in the Chicago *Daily News*. The writer was upset about the false ideas most Americans had about Japan.

Q: Who said, "I feel that I am obliged to make up my mind to pursue unswerving a course that is precisely the opposite of my personal views"?
A: Admiral Yamamoto's personal feelings about conducting a war against the United States.

Q: Who said, "Mr. President, I feel I must tell you that the senior officers of the navy do not have the trust and confidence in the civilian leadership of this country that is essential for a successful prosecution of a war in the Pacific"?
A: Admiral James O. Richardson, then Commander-in-Chief, United States Fleet, said this to President Roosevelt in a conference at the White House in late 1940.

Q: When did Admiral Kimmel make the following statement: I can say only this, that it shall be my personal motto – or guiding principle – to maintain the fleet at the highest level of efficiency and preparedness, and that whatever expansion if ordered, I will attempt to carry out to the best of my ability.
A: It was part of his speech when he became CINCUS on February 1, 1941.

Q: To whom was the comment made, "The last time you were here you hurt the President's feelings"?
A: It was said to Admiral Richardson by Secretary of the Navy Frank Knox in March 1941, in Washington, D.C., when the former asked the Secretary bluntly why he was relieved of command.

Q: Who said, "It appears that the most likely and dangerous form of attack on Oahu would be an air attack...most likely be launched from one or more carriers, probably approach inside of 300 miles...in a dawn attack there is a high probability that it could be delivered as a complete surprise" ?
A: In March 1941, Major General Frederick Martin, commander of the Hawaii

Army Air Corps, and Rear Admiral Patrick L. N. Bellinger, commander of the Hawaii Naval Air Patrol, filed this joint report.

Q: Who wrote, "Operations against the Philippine Islands, Malaya and Dutch East Indies, could not be freely carried out as long as the United States threatened from the rear flanks. America must be so overawed from the start as to cause them to shrink from continuing the war"?
A: Admiral Yamamoto, in January 1941, in a top secret document to his staff officers.

Q: When and how did the United States government first warn Hawaii about a possible attack?
A: Secretary Knox signed a letter on January 24, 1941, warning: "Japan might initiate a surprise attack upon the fleet at Pearl Harbor. Military commanders in Hawaii are to take every step, as quickly as possible, to protect against the attack."

Q: "I sincerely desire to be appointed Commander-in-Chief of the Air Fleet to attack Pearl Harbor so that I may personally command that attack force." Who said this?
A: Admiral Yamamoto's request to Japan's Navy General Staff in January 1941. His request was denied because he was too valuable as the commander of the Combined Fleet.

Q: Who said, "If he has so much confidence, it is better to let Yamamoto go ahead."
A: Admiral Osami Nagano, during the meeting in which Admiral Yamamoto threatened to resign.

Q: Who said, "If we are to have war with America, we will have no hope of winning unless the United States Fleet in Hawaiian waters can be destroyed"?
A: Admiral Yamamoto.

Q: Who said, "He is brusque and undiplomatic in his approach to problems, but he is outstanding in his qualifications of command and this is the opinion of the entire Navy"?
A: Admiral Harold R. Stark, Chief of Naval Operations, gave this description of Admiral Kimmel to General George C. Marshall, Army Chief of Staff, five days after Kimmel became CINCUS.

Q: "A very capable, a very thoroughly grounded and trained officer...he possesses more brains than any other Japanese in high command."
A: This was the opinion of Lieutenant Commander Edwin Layton, Fleet Intelligence, of Admiral Yamamoto, whom he knew personally.

Q: Who said, "If I am told to fight regardless of the consequences, I shall run wild for the first six months or a year, but I have utterly no confidence for the second or third year"?
A: Admiral Yamamoto's answer to Prime Minister Konoye when Konoye approached Yamamoto about a war with the United States and Great

Britain.

Q: What prompted Admiral Yamamoto to make the following statement, "A war between Japan and the United States would be a major calamity for the world, and for Japan it would mean, after several years of war already, acquiring yet another powerful enemy...an extremely perilous matter for the nation"?
A: Although Yamamoto planned the overall attack on Pearl Harbor, he was afraid that a war between Japan and the United States would cause Japan to lose its greatest political asset, its strong navy.

Q: "Here in Hawaii we all live in a citadel or gigantically fortified island." Who said this?
A: Lieutenant General Walter Short, Commanding General, Hawaiian Department, in a speech on April 7, 1941.

Q: Who made the following statement, "Pearl Harbor is the strongest fortress in the world...a major attack is impractical"?
A: In May 1941, Army Chief of Staff, General George C. Marshall, gave this description to President Roosevelt.

Q: Who said, "The activities of Japanese consular officials in Hawaii and the western United States are alarming evidence of the need for a full-scale investigation"?
A: On October 2, 1941, Senator Guy M. Gillette of Iowa introduced this resolution. Nothing was done.

Q: "If the Prime Minister doesn't have the heart for war, he and his cabinet should resign." Who said it?
A: Minister of War General Tojo's demand on October 13, 1941; Prime Minister Prince Konoye resigned.

Q: Who said, "We must strain every nerve to satisfy and keep on good relations with this group of Japanese negotiators. Don't let it deteriorate and break up if you can possibly help it. Let us make no move of ill will. Let us do nothing to precipitate a crisis."
A: President Roosevelt's instructions to Secretary Hull on December 5, 1941.

Q: Who said, "Study the situation at home and abroad without being bound by the Imperial Conference decision of September 6?"
A: This was a last plea from Emperor Hirohito to the Imperial Conference against war.

Q: "...earliest indications of hostilities..."
A: A comment included in a November 4, 1941, intelligence report to Admiral Kimmel about Japanese merchant ships moving out of the western hemisphere.

Q: Who said, "We can't go to war because we aren't ready to go to war"?
A: A statement made by General George C. Marshall shortly before the attack on Pearl Harbor.

Q: Who said, "The success of our surprise attack on Pearl Harbor will prove to be the Waterloo of the war to follow"?
A: Vice Admiral Chuichi Nagumo's prediction to his flag officers on November 10, 1941.

Q: Who said, "Japanese sanity cannot be measured by our standards of logic"?
A: Ambassador Grew's message on 3 November to the United States State Department as he tried to explain Japan's "do or die" attitude, rather than give in to foreign pressure.

Q: What significance did phrases like "...lost German dog named Mayer..." and "...Chinese rugs for sale..." have to Japan?
A: The Japanese Consulate paid for radio advertisements which were broadcasted in the evenings. Announcements such as "...lost German dog named Mayer..." or "...Chinese rugs for sale..." were references to which carrier or warship was in the harbor.

Q: Who said, "If the Emperor intervened, it is known the Japanese people would comply"?
A: Hedenari Terasaki, Ambassador Nomura's personal assistant. On November 29, 1941, Terasaki asked Ambassador Kurusu whether there was someone who could convince President Roosevelt to send a cable directly to Emperor Hirohito, asking for peace. Terasaki meet secretly with Dr. Hu Shih, Chiang Kai-shek's ambassador in D.C. and E. Stanley Jones, a personal friend of Roosevelt. If the meeting was discovered by the Japanese government, Terasaki and his family might have been killed. His actions have made him a hero. Few people knew he was also the head of the Japanese intelligence system. It will probably never be know whether his effort was genuine or a scheme to keep the Americans thinking that there was still time left for peace.

Q: When was the order, "Burn all codes except one each of type O and L. Also burn all secret documents, taking precautions against outside suspicion..." given?
A: Admiral Togo, Foreign Minister, gave this order to Consul Kita, Honolulu Consulate General, on December 2, 1941. Japan discarded the J-19 system and relied upon PA-K2. The PA-K2 code was much simpler for the American intelligence to break. Unfortunately, United States intelligence received copies of Japanese messages from RCA too late to decode before the attack.

Q: Who said, "The United States Navy can defeat the Japanese Navy at any place, at any time"?
A: A statement made by Senator Owen Brewster of Maine while he was at the Naval Air Station in San Juan, Puerto Rico on December 4, 1941.

Q: Who said, "This means war!"?
A: President Roosevelt to Harry Hopkins, his personal advisor. On the evening of December 6, between 2030 and 2045, American decoders had already decoded the first 13 parts of the 14-part message. After reading it, it was clear to Roosevelt that the Japanese were discontinuing further negotia-

tions. When Hopkins suggested that America strike the first blow against Japan, Roosevelt responded, "No, we can't do that. We are a democracy and a peaceful people."

Q: Who said, "The American people may feel fully confident in their Navy...on any comparable basis the United States Navy is second to none"?
A: Secretary of the Navy Frank Knox's report on the United States navy, given on December 6, 1941.

Q: Who made the historic cry, "Tora...tora...tora" (Tiger, tiger, tiger)?
A: Commander Mitsuo Fuchida. Fuchida had control over the air operations once the planes left the carriers. "Tora, tora, tora" was his signal to the carriers that the attack would be a surprise attack.

Q: Who said, "Why don't you pick up the phone and call Admiral Kimmel"?
A: Captain Theodore Wilkinson asked Admiral Stark this question on December 7, at 0900 EST. Captain Wilkinson was Chief of Naval Intelligence, and had just discussed the fourteenth-part of Japan's response to the United States with Admiral Stark. Stark never made the call.

Q: Who sent the following message, "Japanese are presenting on one p.m. eastern standard time today what amounts to an ultimatum. Also they are under orders to destroy their code machines immediately. Just what significance the hour set may have we do not know but be on the alert accordingly. Inform naval authorities of this communication"?
A: A warning message sent by General Marshall, at 1158 Eastern Standard Time on December 7, to Lieutenant General Short.

Q: "Will the ambassador please submit to the United States Government at 1 o'clock p.m. on the 7th your time cutting ties with the United States."
A: The "one o'clock" message sent to Ambassador Nomura from the Japanese Foreign Ministry.

Q: What was the Japanese Embassy to do after deciphering part fourteen and the "one o'clock" message?
A: "Destroy at once the remaining cipher machine and all machine codes."

Q: Who sent this message, "Deepest thanks for your endeavors and hard work"?
A: This was Tokyo's last message to Ambassador Nomura.

Q: Where was this message found, "The bombs which will start the war between Japan and the United States"?
A: This was a message Japanese crewmen painted on bombs dropped during the attack.

Q: Who said "I will fly straight for my objective and make a crash dive into any enemy target rather than an emergency landing"?
A: This was a comment made by a fighter commander when asked what he would do in case of engine failure.

A crashed dive bomber recovered out of the waters of South East Loch.
National Archives

Q: The American Fleet's presence was radioed back to the Japanese Task Force at 0738. What did the message say?
A: "Enemy battleships at anchor at Pearl Harbor. No carriers."

Q: When Lieutenant Outerbridge and a USS *Ward* gunner sighted a submarine in the restricted sea area, what was discussed?
A: The gunner asked, "Captain, what are we going to do?" Outerbridge responded, "We are going to shoot."

Q: Who said, "I have all the confidence in you"?
A: Vice Admiral Nagumo to Commander Fuchida, air commander, shortly before the planes left the carriers.

Q: Who said, "Japanese, man your stations"?
A: Rear Admiral Furlong, as he was standing on deck of his Flagship, USS *Oglala*. He saw a plane drop a bomb near the water's edge off Ford Island. As the plane flew over, he saw "meatballs" on its wings. Furlong sent out a message, "All ships in harbor sortie."

Q: Who sent this message, "Attacked, fired on, depth bombed and sunk submarine operating in defensive sea area"?
A: This message was sent at 0653 from the destroyer USS *Ward* to the Fourteenth Naval District Headquarters.

Q: Who sent the message, "Enemy air raid Pearl Harbor, this is not a drill"?
A: Lieutenant Commander Logan Ramsey at 0758. Immediately afterwards, he sent a second message ordering all planes in the air "to proceed and search 315 degrees to 360 degrees from Pearl Harbor to maximum practical distance." Commander Murphy sent a similar message about the attack a few minutes later to the Chief of Naval Operations (CNO) in Washington, D.C.; to Commander-in-Chief, Asiatic Fleet (CINCAF) in Manila; and to all United States Forces at sea.

Q: Who said, "This is certainly in keeping with their history of surprise attacks"?
A: Captain Mervyn Bennion, captain of the USS *West Virginia*, at the beginning of the attack.

Q: "You wouldn't kid about a thing like that, would you?" Who said it.
A: Rear Admiral Bellinger's response when he was told that the Japanese were attacking Pearl Harbor.

Q: Who said, "My God, they're shooting at my own boys, tell Kimmel"?
A: Vice Admiral Halsey to his Flag Secretary when the message was received about the raid. At 0600 that morning, 18 planes were sent ahead to Pearl Harbor. Halsey thought jittery United States gunners had opened up on his planes.

Q: Who ordered, "Locate enemy force"?
A: This was Admiral Kimmel's first order after the attack started. It was given to Patrol Wing Two at 0817.

Q: Who said, "The smoke and flames erupted together. It was a hateful, mean looking red flame, the kind that powder produces, and I knew at once that a big powder magazine had exploded"?
A: Commander Fuchida's description of the explosion of the USS *Arizona*.

USS *Arizona*. National Archives

Q: Who said, "He groaned like a man under torture"?
A: Vice Admiral Pye's description of Admiral Kimmel when Pye informed him about the damage on Battleship Row.

Q: "Pearl Harbor! It should be our strongest point." Who said this?
A: General Douglas MacArthur's first reaction after learning of the attack.

Q: Who announced, "Hostilities with Japan commenced with air raid on Pearl Harbor"?
A: This announcement was made by CINCUS Headquarters at 0816 to all American ships and stations.

Q: "Joy and gratification filled my heart at the time, for I knew our mission would be a success." Who said it?
A: Commander Fuchida's reflections on the attack.

Q: Who said, "Bombed Ford Island, Hickam and Wheeler, terrible damage inflicted"?
A: Pilot Takabashi radioed this message back to the *Akagi*.

Brigadier General Jacob Rudolph's personal B-18 at Hickam. National Archives

Q: "You can land at Hickam, but there are three Japs on your tail and the anti-aircraft fire is erratic and dangerous." What was this?
A: A message received aboard the in-coming B-17's on their approach to Oahu at the beginning of the attack.

Q: "There's a message from the signal tower saying the Japanese are attacking Pearl Harbor and this is not a drill." Who said this?
A: While Commander Murphy was talking by phone with Admiral Kimmel, and reporting the USS *Ward* sightings, his yeoman burst in on him with this message.

Q: When was the message, "Japanese submarine in harbor" sent?
A: At 0832, Admiral Kimmel's headquarters sent this alert to all ships.

Q: When was the announcement, "All military personnel are under orders to return to their stations immediately" made?
A: KGMB Radio Station made this announcement at 0804, then went back to playing music. The station repeated the announcement again at 0805 and 0830. It was not until 0840 that it announced that an attack was in progress.

Q: How did the radio station finally get the attention of the residents that an attack was occurring?
A: Webly Edwards, a broadcaster with KGMB, made the announcement, "This is the real McCoy."

Q: Who said, "Praise the lord and pass the ammunition"?
A: Chaplain Howell Forgy, when the power went off aboard the USS *New Orleans* and the ammunition lifts stopped. That phrase also inspired one of the war's most favorite songs.

Q: Who said, "That's ridiculous"?
A: Lieutenant General Short's outburst when Lieutenant George Bicknell told him he had just seen two battleships sunk.

Q: "Stay in there and pitch, Walter." Who said it?
A: Mrs. Short's encouragement to her husband, Lieutenant General Short, when they were in the shelter tunnel at Fort Shafter.

Q: "War! Oahu Bombed By Japanese Planes"
A: The headline for the *Star Bulletin*'s special edition.

Q: Who said, "I believe I'm losing the power to make a decision"?
A: Major General Martin, Commander, Hawaiian Air Force's statement to his chief of staff on the morning of December 7. Later that day, Martin's chief of staff put Martin in Hickam Field hospital.

Q: Who said, "I was instructed to deliver at 1:00"?
A: This was Ambassador Nomura's apology when he met with Secretary Hull. He told Hull that he did not know why he was told to deliver the fourteen part message at 1:00 p.m., but that was his instruction. Ambassador Nomura had not yet heard of the attack.

Q: "In fifty years of public service, I have never seen a document more crowded with infamous falsehoods and distortions."
A: This was Secretary Hull's response to Ambassador Nomura when Nomura delivered Japan's fourteenth-part message to Secretary Hull. Hull did not know Nomura was unaware of the attack.

Q: Who ordered, "Rendezvous as directed by Command Task Force 8"?
A: At 0921, CINCUS radioed this order to all ships and forces afloat.

Q: While Admiral Kimmel watched the attack from his office, a stray a .50 caliber machine gun bullet broke his window and struck him in the chest. The bullet had lost most of its force and fell to the ground without injuring Kimmel. As Kimmel bent to pick it up, what did he say?
A: "It would have been merciful had it killed me."

Q: Why was the USS *West Virginia* described as "a ship burning like a forest fire"?
A: When the USS *West Virginia* had been repainted, each new coat was painted over the old coat. The thick layer of paint, mixed with turpentine, readily burned

USS *West Virginia* and USS *Tennessee*. National Archives

Q: Who said, "I won't issue supplies without a signed receipt"?
A: A supply master on Ford Island. In the lull between attacks, men started to cannibalize planes and get them into the air to search for the Japanese carriers. When Rear Admiral Patrick Bellinger was told that the supply master was not going to give out supplies, he took a group of Marines, led then to the supply room, and ordered them to take what they wanted.

Q: "It was so large in fact, that I checked the equipment to determine whether it was the fault of the equipment or actually a flight of some sort." Who said it?
A: Private Lockard's description of what he did when he spotted what appeared to be planes coming in on December 7 on his radar.

Q: "We have reason to believe that they (the Japanese) lost a complete squadron on account of the message the Navy picked up from a squadron commander sent in to his carrier saying that he was lost and he was out of gas; so there is a possibility that there was a complete squadron lost in addition to what was brought down." Who said it?
A: Lieutenant General Short reported this after hearing about a plane going down. It was a lost dive bomber trying to return to the *Zuikaku*. The carrier would not break radio silence. When the bomber ran out of fuel, the crew told the carrier they were going down and shouted "bonzai" as they crashed.

Q: Who said, "Did you get my message"?
A: General Marshall to Colonel Phillips, Lieutenant General Short's chief of staff, when Phillips called him in Washington, D. C. to tell him about the attack.

Q: Who said, "That radio operator who was transmitting as if he was kicking it with his foot"?
A: Commander Joseph J. Rochefort, head of the Pearl Harbor Intelligence Unit's description of how naval intelligence knew the Japanese flagship *Akagi* was part of the attack.

Q: "Somebody is flashing a bright signal at Lualualei which can be seen at sea. Signal for enemy landing parties." What was this?
A: A report made after the attack. The light turned out to be moonlight shining on the tin roof of a Portuguese laborer's house.

Q: What prompted reports of "Enemy troops landing on North Shore,", "paratroopers landing on Barbers Point"?
A: They were triggered by a mechanic in dungarees who parachuted after his seaplane was shot down by Americans.

Q: Who said, "Before we're through with them, the Japanese language will be spoken only in Hell"?
A: Vice Admiral William F. "Bull" Halsey.

Q: Who said, "Its nothing but a God-damn mousetrap"?
A: Admiral Richardson's comment to President Roosevelt, before Richardson was relieved of command.

Q: Who said, "The damn thing won't do any good now"?
A: Colonel Dunlop, at Lieutenant General Short's Headquarters at 1458 on December 7, when he read General Marshall's message warning Hawaii about a potential attack.

Q: What prompted Admiral Kimmel to say, "Oh what a doleful sight"?
A: This was his response when Major General Howard C. Davidson tried to cheer Kimmel up by telling he hadn't lost too much, "just some old battleships and few other craft. You still have your carriers and cruisers."

Q: Who said, "My greatest mistake was being captured. This is the first time I have failed. Please do not advise Japan about this. Please kill me"?
A: Ensign Kazuo Sakamaki, America's first Japanese prisoner of war's request when captured.

Q: What was considered "the best ship in the Pacific Fleet"?
A: The USS *West Virginia*. It was affectionately referred to as "WEEVEE".

Q: Who sent the message, "Today all of us are in the same boat with you, the people of the empire, and it is a ship which will not and cannot be sunk"?
A: President Roosevelt sent this cable to Winston Churchill immediately after Congress passed the resolution to declare war on Japan.

Q: Who said, "If I were in charge in Washington, I would relieve Kimmel at once. It doesn't make any difference why a man fails in the Navy, he has failed"?
A: Admiral Kimmel told this to two of his subordinates. He understood the Navy's philosophy that the captain of a ship is responsible for anything that happens within his command.

Q: "Now the only reason why I write this is the feeling that some Admiral or some General in the Pacific may be made a goat for action or lack of action higher up, and thus a great injustice done." Who said it?
A: Former President Herbert Hoover wrote this to his friend, Major General Frank McCoy, when he learned that McCoy had been appointed to the Roberts Commission.

Q: "You have my sympathy. The same thing would have happened to anybody." Who said it?
A: Admiral Nimitz's condolences to Admiral Kimmel, upon his arrival at Pearl Harbor to take over the Fleet Command.

Q: Who reported, "I have never seen the Fleet in a higher state of readiness..."?
A: Admiral Stanley's statement to Secretary Knox immediately after the attack on Pearl Harbor. Because Stanley realized the Fleet was ready for battle, Stanley was sorry he had to recommend that Kimmel be relieved. The relief was purely for political reasons.

Q: "A more disgraceful spectacle has never been presented to this country during my lifetime than the failure of the civilian officials of the government to show any willingness to take their share of responsibility for the Japanese success of Pearl Harbor..." Who said this?
A: Admiral J. O. Richardson to Admiral Kimmel when he found out the results of the Roberts Commission.

Q: Who reported, "never at any time prior, during or subsequent to the attack"?
A: The FBI agent in charge in Hawaii reported this to congressional investigating committees after the war, when he was asked about the existence of sab-

otage or fifth column activity in Hawaii.

Q: Who said, "Immediately after the attack on Pearl Harbor, I felt that no matter how hard and how conscientiously I had tried, I had not been smart enough and to that extent, must accept blame for Pearl Harbor"?
A: Admiral Husband Kimmel.

Q: Who said, "Every circumstance of calculated and characteristic Japanese treachery was employed"?
A: Winston Churchill, addressing the House of Commons on December 8, 1941.

Q: "I promise you final victory." Who said it?
A: General Tojo, addressing the media after the attack.

Q: Who said "We cannot lose the war, now we have a partner who has not been defeated in 3,000 years"?
A: Adolph Hitler's excited statement when he heard the news that Pearl Harbor was bombed.

Q: "...the printed report does not and could not go into what is the real underlying basis of the trouble, namely that both services had not fully learned the lessons of the development of air power in respect to the defense of a navy and of a naval base." Who said it?
A: Secretary Stimson in his reaction to the Roberts Commission report.

Q: "As long as he behaved like a tourist and stayed off government property, he was safe." Who said it?
A: Head of the Honolulu FBI, Agent Robert Shivers, years later, explaining why the Japanese spy Morimura was not arrested.

Q: "If they were surprised by the news from Pearl Harbor, then that group of elderly men were putting on a performance which would have excited the admiration of any experienced actor." Who wrote this?
A: Edward R. Murrow, announcer for the Columbia Broadcasting Systems Communications, describing his evening at the White House on December 7, 1941.

Q: "Since learning the definite information of the Japanese intention to attack United States was in the hands of War and Navy Department and was not supplied to me, I now refuse to accept any responsibility for the catastrophe." Who said it?
A: Admiral Husband Kimmel.

Q: Who said, "The attack was like a dog biting a hand, not a fatal blow."
A: Admiral Yamamoto used that description about the attack to his officers, since he knew Japan could not win a long war with the United States and he didn't think Japan had the political know-how to negotiate a settlement that would help Japan.

Q: "The basic trouble was that the Navy failed to appreciate what the Japanese could do and did do." Who said it?
A: Admiral Ernest King at the inquiries after the war.

Q: "...I am afraid we have awakened a sleeping giant..."
A: Admiral Yamamoto's prophetic comment about the impact the attack on Pearl Harbor would have on the outcome of the war.

DECLARATION OF WAR

Yesterday, December 7, 1941 – a date which will live in infamy – the United States of America was suddenly and deliberately attacked by the naval and air forces of the Empire of Japan.

The United States was at peace with that Nation and, at the solicitation of Japan, was still in conversation with its Government and its Emperor looking toward the maintenance of peace in the Pacific. Indeed, one hour after Japanese air squadrons had commenced bombing in Oahu, the Japanese Ambassador to the United States and his colleague delivered to the Secretary of State a formal reply to a recent American message. While this reply stated that it seemed useless to continue the existing diplomatic negotiations, it contained no threat or hint of war or armed attack.

It will be recorded that the distance of Hawaii from Japan makes it obvious that the attack was deliberately planned many days or even weeks ago. During the intervening time the Japanese Government has deliberately sought to deceive the United States by false statements and expressions of hope for continued peace.

The attack yesterday on the Hawaiian Islands has caused severe damage to American naval and military forces. Very many American lives have been lost. In addition American ships have been reported torpedoed on the high seas between San Francisco and Honolulu.

Yesterday the Japanese Government also launched an attack against Malaya.

Last night Japanese forces attacked Hong Kong.

Last night Japanese forces attacked Guam.

Last night Japanese forces attacked Wake Island.

This morning the Japanese attacked Midway Island.

Japan has, therefore, undertaken a surprise offensive extending throughout the Pacific area. The facts of yesterday speak for themselves. The people of the United States have already formed their opinions and well understand the implications to the very life and safety of our Nation.

As Commander-in-Chief of the Army and Navy I have directed that all measures be taken for our defense.

Always will we remember the character of the onslaught against us.

No matter how long it may take us to overcome this premeditated invasion, the American people in their righteous might will win through to absolute victory.

I believe I interpret the will of the Congress and of the people when I assert that we will not only defend ourselves to the uttermost but will make very certain that this form of treachery shall never endanger us again.

Hostilities exist. There is no blinking at the fact that our people, our territory, and our interests are in grave danger.

With confidence in our armed forces – with the unbounded determination of our people – we will gain the inevitable triumph – so help us God.

I ask that Congress declare that since the unprovoked and dastardly attack by Japan on Sunday, December seventh, a state of war has existed between the United States and the Japanese Empire.

Delivered by President Roosevelt on December 8, 1941, to Congress.

President Roosevelt addressing Congress. National Archives

Appendix A

U.S. SHIPS AT PEARL HARBOR
ON THE MORNING OF DECEMBER 7, 1941

Allen(DD-66)
Antares(AKS-3)
Argonne(AG-31)
Arizona(BB-39)
Ash(YN-2)
Avocet(AVP-4)
Aylwin(DD-355)
Bagley(DD-386)
Blue(DD-387)
Bobolink(AM-20)
Breese(DM-18)
Cachelot(SS-17-)
California(BB-44)
Case(DD-370)
Cassin(DD-372)
Castor(AKS-1)
CG-8(USCG)
Chengho(IX-52)
Chew(DD-106)
Cinchona(YN-7)
Cockatoo(AMc-8)
Cockenoe(YN-47)
Condor(AMc-14)
Conyngham(DD-371)
Crossbill(AMc-9)
Cummings(DD-365)
Curtiss(AV-4)
Dale(DD-353)
Detroit(CL-8)
Dewey(DD349)
Dobbin(AD-3)
Dolphin(SS-169)
Downes(DD-375)
Farragut(DD-348)
Gamble(DM-15)
Grebe(AM-43)
Helena(CL-50)
Helm(DD-388)
Henley(DD-391)
Hoga(YT-146)
Honolulu(CL-48)
West Virginia(BB-48)
Whitney(AD-4)
Widgeon(ASR-1)
Worden(DD-352)
YG-15
YG-17
YG-21
YMT-5

Hulbert(AVD-6)
Hull(DD-350)
Jarvis(DD-393)
Keosangua(AT-38)
MacDonough(DD-351)
Manuwai(YFB-17)
Marin(YN-53)
Maryland(BB-46)
Medusa(AR-1)
Monaghan(DD-354)
Montgomery(DM-17)
Mugford(DD-389)
Narwhal(SS-167)
Navajo(AT-64)
Neosho(AO-23)
Nevada(BB-36)
New Orleans(CA-32)
Nokomis(YT-142)
Oglala(CM-4)
Oklahoma(BB-37)
Ontario(AT-13)
Osceola(YT-129)
Patterson(DD-392)
Pelias(AS-14)
Pennsylvania(BB-38)
Perry(DMS-17)
Phelps(DD-360)
Phoenix(CL-46)
Preble(DM-20)
Pruitt(DM-22)
PT-20
PT-21
PT-22
PT-23
PT-24
PT-25
PT-26
PT-27
PT-28
PT-29
PT-30
YNg-17
YO-21
YO-43
YP-108
YP-109
YT-3
YT-119
YT-30

PT-42
Pyro(AE-1)
Rail(AM-1)
Raleigh(CL-7)
Ralph Talbot(DD-390
Ramapo(AO-12)
Ramsay(DM-16)
Reedbird(AMc-30)
Reid(DD-369)
Reliance(USCG)
Reigel(AR-11)
Sacramento(PG-19)
St. Louis(CL-49)
San Francisco(CA-38)
Schley(DD-103)
Selfridge(DD-357)
Shaw(DD-373)
Sicard(DM-21)
Solace(AH-5)
Sotoyomo(YT-9)
Sumner(AG-32)
Sunnadin(AT-28)
Swan(AVP-7)
Taney(PG-37)(USCG)
Tangier(AV-8)
Tautog(SS-199)
Tennessee(BB-43)
Tern(AM-31)
Thornton(AVD-11)
Tiger(PC-152)(USCG)
Tracy(DM-19)
Trever(DMS-16)
Tucker(DD-374)
Turkey(AM-13)
Utah(AG-16)
Vega(AK-17)
Vestal(AR-4)
Vireo(AM-52)
Wapello(YN-56)
Ward(DD-139)
Wasmuth(DMS-15)
YT-152
YT-153
YW-16
Zane(DMS-14)
YO-30
YO-40

Appendix B

HAWAII OPERATION TASK FORCE

AERIAL ATTACK

1st Carrier Division
   Akagi
   Kaga

2nd Carrier Division
   Soryu
   Hiryu

5th Carrier Division
   Zuikaku
   Shokaku

1st Destroyer Squadron
   Abukuma (light cruiser)
   17th Destroyer Division
     Tanikaze
     Urakaze
     Isokaze
     Hamakaze
   18th Destroyer Division
     Kasumi
     Arare
     Kagero
     Shiranuhi
     Akigumo

3rd Battleship Division
   Hiei
   Kirishima

8th Cruiser Division
   Tone
   Chikuma

2nd Submarine Division
   I-19
   I-21
   I-23

7th Destroyer Division
   Akebono
   Ushio

1st Supply Train
   Kyokuto Maru
   Kenyo Maru
   Kokuyo Maru
   Shinkoku Maru
   Akebono Maru

2nd Supply Train
   Toho Maru
   Toei Maru
   Nihon Maru

SUBMARINE ATTACK

Katori (cruiser)

1st Submarine Squadron
   I-9
   I-15
   I-17
   I-25

2nd Submarine Squadron
   I-7   I-4
   I-1   I-5
   I-2   I-6
   I-3

3rd Submarine Squadron
   I-8   I-75
   I-68 I-16
   I-69 I-18
   I-70 I-20
   I-71 I-22
   I-72 I-24
   I-73 I-10
   I-74 I-26

Appendix C
MEDAL OF HONOR RECIPIENTS
December 7, 1941

Name	Unit
*Bennion, Mervyn S. Capt. USN	USS *West Virginia*
Finn, John W. Avn. Ord. Mate, USN	Naval Air Station Kaneohe Bay
*Flaherty, Francis C. Ens. USN	USS *Oklahoma*
Fuqua, Samuel G. Lt. Comdr., USN	USS *Arizona*
*Hammerberg, Owen F.P. BM 2, USN	Salvage Unit Pacific Fleet
*Hill, Edwin J. BMC., USN	USS *Nevada*
*Jones, Herbert C. Ens., USN	USS *California*
*Kidd, Isaac C. Rear Adm, USN	USS *Arizona*
Pharris, Jackson C. GMC, USN	USS *California*
*Reeves, Thomas J. Radio Elec., USN	USS *California*
Ross, Donald K. WO Mach., USN	USS *Nevada*
*Scott, Robert R. MM1, USN	USS *California*
*Tomich, Peter WTC, USN	USS *Utah*
*Van Valkenburg, Franklin Capt., USN	USS *Arizona*
*Ward, James R. S1c., USN	USS *Oklahoma*
Young, Cassin Comdr., USN	USS *Vestal*

*Posthumously Awarded

BIBLIOGRAPHY

Agawa, Hioryuki. *The Reluctant Admiral, Yamamoto And The Imperial Navy.* Tokyo:Kodansha, 1979.

Beekman, Alan. *The Niihau Incident.* Honolulu:Heritage Press of the Pacific, 1982.

Behr, Edward. *Hirohito, Behind The Myth.* New York:Villard Books, 1989.

Browne, Courtney. *Tojo: The Last Banzai.* New York:Holt, Rinehart and Winston, 1967.

Bradley, John H. *The Second World War, Asia And The Pacific.* Wayne, Avery Publishing Group Inc., 1989.

Calvocoressi, Peter and Wint, Guy. *Total War.* New York:Pantheon Books, 1972.

Cleary, Thomas. *The Japanese Art Of War.* Boston:Shambhala, 1991.

Evans, David C. *The Japanese Navy In World War II.* Annapolis,MD:Naval Institute Press, 1969.

Feis, Herbert. *The Road To Pearl Harbor.* Princeton, NJ:Princeton University Press, 1950.

Hoyt, Edwin P. *Japan's War, The Great Pacific Confict.* New York:McGraw Hill, 1986.

Hoyt, Edwin P. *America's Wars & Military Excursions.* New York:McGraw Hill, 1987.

Kennedy, Paul. *The Rise and Fall Of The Great Powers.* New York:Random House, 1987.

Lord, Walter. *Day Of Infamy.* New York:Holt, Reinhart & Co., 1957.

Larrabee, Eric. *Commander in Chief.* New York:Harper & Row, 1987.

Layton, Rear Admiral Edwin T.(RET) and Costello, John. *"And I Was There" Pearl Harbor and Midway-Breaking The Secrets.* New York:Morrow, 1985.

Leckie, Robert. *The Wars Of America.* New York:Harper & Row, 1981.

MacArthur, Douglas. *Reminiscences.* New York:McGraw Hill, 1964.

Manchester, William. *American Caesar.* Boston:Little Brown, 1978.

Manning, Paul. *Hirohito, The War Years.* New York:Dodd, Mead & Co., 1986.

Morrison, Samuel. *The Rising Sun In The Pacifc.* Boston:Little Brown, 1948.

Morgan, Ted. *FDR, A Biography.* New York:Simon and Schuster, 1985.

Murphy, Edward F. *Heros Of World War II.* Novato, CA:Presidio Press, 1990.

Potter, E.B. *Nimitz.* Annapolis, MD:Naval Institute Press, 1987.

Prange, Gordon W. *At Dawn We Slept.* New York:McGraw Hill, 1981.

Prange, Gordon W. *Pearl Harbor, The Verdict Of History.* New York:McGraw Hill,

1986.

Prange, Gordon W. *Dec. 7, 1941, The Day The Japanese Attacked Pearl Harbor.* New York:McGraw Hill, 1988.

Prange, Gordon W. *God's Samurai, Lead Pilot At Pearl Harbor.* Washington:Brassey's (U.S.) Inc., 1990.

Rusbridger, James and Nave, Eric. *Betrayal At Pearl Harbor.* New York:Summit Books, 1991.

Sperber, A.M. *Murrow, His Life And Times.* NewYork:Freundlich Books, 1986.

Stillwell, Paul. *Air Raid Pearl Harbor! Recollections Of A Day Of Infamy.* New York:Naval Institute Press, 1981.

Toland, John. *Infamy.* New York:Berkley Publishing Group, 1983.

Takaki, Ronald. *Strangers From A Different Shore, A History Of Asian Americans.* Boston:Little Brown, 1989.

Thompson, Robert Smith. *A Time For War.* New York:Prentice Hall Press, 1991.

INDEX

ABC-1, 13
Akagi, carrier, 31, 46, 47, 52, 55, 88, 116
Akui, Sergeant David, 80
Alphabetical Typewriter, 39
Andrews, Vice Admiral Adolphus, 23
Antares, supply ship, 56
Anti-Cominter, 5
Arizona, battleship, 21, 62, 65, 67, 68, 69, 70, 71, 95, 96, 97, 112
Armaments Appropriations Act, 6
Arnold, "Hap", 33
Australian Special Intelligence, 44
Aylwin, battleship, 68

Battle of Niihau, 93
Battle of the Tank Farm, 95
Bellinger, Rear Admiral Patrick L. N., 107, 112, 115
Bennion, Captain Mervyn, 70, 112
Bicknell, Lieutenant Colonel George, 114
Bishop, Max, 11
Bloch, Rear Admiral Claude, 28, 32, 40
"bomb message", 43
Bode, Captain H. D., 43
Brewster, Senator Owen, 109
Briggs, Ralph, 44
Brooks, Ensign Roland, 84
Bunkley, Captain J. W., 70, 81
Bushido, 22
Bywater, Hector, 23

Cachelot, submarine, 69
California, battleship, 62, 69, 81, 82, 96
Cate, Philip, 38

Central Intelligence Agency (CIA), 104
Chiang Kai-shek, 4, 10, 14, 109
Chikuma, heavy cruiser, 52,
Chinese Exclusion Act of 1882, 3
China Incident, 22
Churchill, Winston, 14, 102, 117, 118
CINCUS, 25, 34, 106, 113, 114
Clark, Carter, 101
Columbia Broadcasting System, 43, 118
Combat Intelligence Unit, 39
Commerce, Treaty of, 5
Condor, minesweeper, 52, 76
Coolidge, President Calvin, 3
Crossbill, minesweeper, 76
Currier, "Wimpy", 38
Curtiss, seaplane tender, 77, 80, 87, 95
Cynthia Olsen, schooner, 97

Davidson, Major General Howard C., 116
Delany, Captain Walter, 25
Department of Defense, 104
Detroit, light cruiser, 89
Dolphin, submarine, 69
Downes, destroyer, 95
Draemel, Rear Admiral Milo F., 70, 89
Driscoll, Agnes, 38
Dunlop, Colonel Robert H., 116

Early, Stephan, 98
"East-Wind-Rain", 44
Edwards, Webly, 114
Egusa, Lieutenant Commander Takashige, 78
Elliott, Private George E, 56
Emmons, Lieutenant General Delos C., 100

Enterprise, carrier, 33, 59, 65, 86, 87, 88, 90, 92
Essentials of the Policy toward South Seas, 9
Eta Jima Naval Academy, 30

Farthing, Colonel William, 69
Federal Bureau of Investigation, 41, 87, 95, 118
Federal Communications Act of 1934, 41
"Fifth Column", 41, 42, 92
Fillmore, Millard, 1
Forgy, Chaplain Howell, 114
Forrestal, Secretary of the Navy James, 101
Friedman, William, 38
Fuchida, Commander Mitsuo, 55, 57, 59, 63, 70, 110, 112, 113
Furlong, Rear Admiral William, 87, 111
Fuqua, Lieutenant Commander Samuel, 71

Gabrielson, William A., 18
Genda, Commander Minoru, 27, 28, 84, 88
Gillette, Senator Guy M., 108
"Gobbledygook", 44
"grab list", 94
Grand Joint Exercise Number Four, 21
Grew, Ambassador Joseph C., 11, 12, 16, 99, 105, 109

Haan, Kilsoo, 43, 44
Halsey, Vice Admiral William, 26, 29, 33, 112, 116
Harding, President Warren, 3
Hawaii Naval Air Patrol, 107
Hawaii Operation, 13, 27, 28, 31, 39
Hawaiian Army Air Corps, 25, 32, 35, 61, 63, 85, 95, 106
Hawaiian Department, 22, 26, 94

Hawaiian Detachment, 22
Hawley-Smoot Tariff of 1930, 3
Helena, cruiser, 47, 63, 95
Helm, destroyer, 68, 95
Herron, Major General Charles D., 28
Hiei, 44
Hirohito, Emperor, 13, 16, 34, 35, 95, 108
Hiryu, carrier, 46, 47
Hitler, Adolph, 118
Honolulu, light cruiser, 77, 95
Honolulu International Airport, 103
Hoover, President Herbert, 117
Hoover, J. Edgar, 43
Hopkins, Harry, 109
Hornbeck, Stanley D., 10, 11
Hosogaya, Vice Admiral Hoshiro, 48
Hu Shih, Chinese Ambassador, 14, 109
Hulbert, destroyer, 62
Hull, Secretary of State Cordell, 4, 10, 11, 12, 14, 15, 97, 114
Hull Note, 14, 15
"Hypo" Station, 39, 86

Iida, Lieutenant Fusata, 60
Imperial Fifth Fleet, 48
Imperial Naval College, 40
Imperial Policy, 12
Iolani Palace, 89
Itaya, Lieutenant Commander Shigeru, 55
Ito, Captain Risaburo, 39

J-19, 38
Jagersfontein, liner, 79
Japanese Consulate, 41, 42, 43, 49, 82, 93, 97
Japanese Embassy, 17
Japanese Naval Intelligence, 38, 40

Japanese Navy Secret Operation Code, 38
Japanese Naval War College, 30, 40
Jimmu, Emperor, 1
JN-25, 37, 38, 103
Jones, Private James, 104
Jones, E. Stanley, 109
Jupiter, collier, 21

Kaga, carrier, 46, 47
Kaleohano, Howard, 93
Kanahele, Benjamin, 93
Kanai, Petty Officer Noboru, 70
"Katamichi Kogeki", 29
Kellogg-Briand Non-Aggression Pact, 3
Kidd, Rear Admiral Isaac C., 70
"Kido Butai", 45, 50
Kimmel, Admiral Husband E., 25, 26, 28, 29, 32, 33, 34, 44, 48, 49, 62, 66, 68, 78, 89, 92, 100, 101, 102, 103, 106, 108, 112, 115, 116, 117, 118
King, Admiral Ernest, 119
Kingdom of Hawaii, 19
Kita, Consul General Nagao, 12, 87
Knox, Secretary of the Navy Frank, 99, 107, 110, 117
Konoye, Prime Minister Fumimaro, 12, 13, 107
Kublai Khan, 1
Kuehn, Bernard, 42, 99
Kurusu, Saburo, 12, 15, 16, 109
Kwangtung Army, 21

Lang Son Incident, 23
Langley, carrier, 21
Lanikai, 49
Layton, Lieutenant Commander Edwin T., 39, 107
Lea, Homer, 23
League of Nations, 3, 4

Leary, Rear Admiral H. Fairfax, 70
Lexington, carrier, 21, 59
Lockard, Private Joseph L., 56, 115
London Naval Conference of 1930, 3
Lurline, ocean liner, 44, 48, 49
Lytton Report, 4

MacArthur, General Douglas, 101, 113
"magic", 39, 101
Mahan, Admiral Alfred T., 20
Major Disaster Council, 90
Mao Tse-Tung, 4
Marco Polo Bridge, 22
Martial law, 93, 94
Martin, Major General Frederick, 32, 63, 106, 114
Martin, Commander Harold, 69, 84
Marshall, General George C., 17, 18, 33, 101, 108, 110, 116
Maryland, battleship, 73, 90, 96
Matsuoka, Foreign Minister Yosuke, 6, 12
Mayfield, Captain Irving, 39, 41
McCoy, Major General Frank, 117
Meiji Constitution, 6
Meyer, Agnes, 38
Miller, Mess Attendant Doris, 74
Mitchell, General Billy, 105
Model SCR-270, 32
Monaghan, destroyer, 68, 76, 77, 97
Montgomery, destroyer-minelayer, 80
Moral embargo, 5
Morimura, Tadashi, 118
Murray, Major General Maxwell, 63
Murata, Lieutenant Commander Shigeharu, 55

Murphy, Commander Vincent, 112, 113
Murrow, Edward R., 118

Nagano, Admiral Osami, 7
Nagato, battleship, 32
Nagumo, Vice Admiral Chuichi, 30, 31, 33, 41, 44, 46, 48, 49, 53, 55, 66, 88, 91, 92, 103, 109, 111
Nakamura, General Akito, 23
Narwhal, submarine, 69
National Defense Act, 6
Navy Code D, 37
Neosho, tanker, 74
Neutrality Acts, 4
Nevada, battleship, 62, 80, 82, 84, 96
New Orleans, heavy cruiser, 77, 114
Nimitz, Admiral Chester W., 21, 102, 117
Nishikaichi, Pilot Shigenori, 93
Nomura, Ambassador Kichisaburo, 12, 14, 15, 16, 18, 19, 33, 99, 103, 110, 114
Nonaggression Pact of 1928, 16
Non-Recognition Doctrine of 1932, 4
Northhampton, cruiser, 88
Noyes, Rear Admiral Leigh, 44

Ogawa, Captain Kanji, 11, 40, 43
Oglala, minelayer, 81, 95, 111
Oklahoma, battlehip, 60, 64, 65, 66, 73, 96
Okuda, Vice Consul Otojiro, 87
Onishi, Rear Admiral Takijiro, 27
OP-12, 43
OP-20-G, 36, 37, 38, 44
Open Door Policy, 2, 3, 14
Operation Z, 28
Orange Plan, 28
Organized Defense Volunteers, 98

Outerbridge, Lieutenant William, 111

Panay, gunboat, 5, 22
Patton, General George S., 22
Pearl Harbor Intelligence Unit, 39
Perry, Commodore Matthew G., 1, 11
Pennsylvania, battleship, 49, 82, 83, 90, 96
Petrie, Lester, Mayor of Honolulu, 18
Phillips, Lieutenant Colonel Walter, 77, 116
Phoenix, light cruiser, 89
Pineapple Fleet, 23
Plan Dog, 24
Poindexter, Governor Joseph B., 18, 87, 89
Popov, Dusko, 43
Port Arthur Incident, 20
Portland, cruiser, 88
Portsmouth Treaty, 20
Proclamation 2525, 98
Proposal B, 14
Purple machine, 38, 44
Pye, Vice Admiral William S., 28, 29, 113

"Quarantine" speech, 5
"Queens of the Seas", 26
Quota Act of 1924, 2

Rainbow 5, 13, 27
Raleigh, light cruiser, 60, 95
Ramsay, Lieutenant Commander Logan, 112
Ranneft, Captain Johan E., 44
RCA, 18, 97
Reciprocity Treaty, 19
Richardson, Admiral James O., 24, 106, 116, 117
Rivera-Schreiber, Richardo, 11

Robalo, submarine, 101
Roberts Commission, 100, 117
Roberts, Owen J., 100
Rochefort, Commander Joseph J., 39, 116
Rodgers Field, 62, 103
Roosevelt, President Franklin D., 5, 9, 12, 14, 15, 24, 25, 98, 100, 105, 108, 109, 119
Roosevelt, President Theodore, 20
Rudolph, Brigadier General Jacob, 113
Russo-Japanese War, 2, 20, 21, 29

Safford, Commander Lawrence F., 36, 37, 38, 44
Sakamaki, Ensign Kazuo, 80, 117
Sakamoto, Lieutenant Akira, 63
Saratoga, carrier, 21, 59
Sarnoff, David, 41
Scanland, Captain F. W., 70
Selective Training and Service Act, 6
Sevareid, Eric, 43
Shaw, destroyer, 80, 95
Shimada, Vice Admiral Shigetaro, 8, 9
Shimazaki, Lieutenant Commander Shigekazu, 78, 95
Shindo, Lieutenant Saburo, 78
Shivers, Robert, 87, 118
Shoemaker, Captain James H., 69
Shokaku, carrier, 46, 47, 56
Short, Lieutenant General Walter C., 26, 28, 32, 43, 88, 100, 101, 102, 103, 108, 114, 116
Sino-Japanese War, 2, 6, 21
Sino-Korean People's League, 43
Solace, hospital ship, 82
Soryu, carrier, 46, 47, 70
Sotoyomo, tugboat, 80, 95
Spanish American War, 37, 96
Stark, Admiral Harold, 24, 25, 28, 33, 107, 110

Stimson Doctrine, 4
Stimson, Henry, 9, 10, 98, 100, 101, 118
St. Louis, light cruiser, 87, 89

Tachibana, Lieutenant Commander Itaru, 40
Taiyo Maru, 41
Takahashi, Lieutenant Commander Kakuichi, 55
"Target A", 75
Tatuta Maru, 12, 91
Taussig, Ensign Joseph, 77
Tautog, submarine, 69
Taylor, Lieutenant Kenneth, 81
Tennessee, battleship, 74, 77, 90, 96
Terasaki, Hidenari, 109
Territory of Hawaii, 16
Toei Maru, 47
Togo, Admiral Heihachiro, 20, 28
Togo, Foreign Minister Shigenori, 15, 16, 17, 103, 109
Tojo, General Hideki, 7, 8, 12, 13, 15, 108, 118
Tone, heavy cruiser, 52
Toyoda, Vice Admiral Teijiro, 12
Trade Agreements Act of 1934, 4
Tripartite Pact, 5, 6
Tyler, Lieutenant Kermit, 56

"ultra", 39
Underwood Code machine, 37
U.S. Army Signal Intelligence (SIS), 37, 38
U.S. Military Intelligence, 37
U.S. Naval Communication Service, 36, 38
U.S. Navy Foreign Intelligence, 43
U.S. Navy Office of Naval Intelligence (ONI), 37, 38, 43, 44
Utah, target ship, 34, 60, 65, 70, 95

Van Valkenburg, Captain Franklin, 70
Versailles, Treaty of, 3
Vestal, repair ship, 67, 68, 95
Vichy Government, 9

Walker, Colonel Eugene, 72
Wallace, Vice President Henry, 18
War Department Signal Center, 18
Ward, destroyer, 52, 56, 62, 111, 113
WARDS (Women Air Raid Defense), 98
Washington Naval Conference of 1921-22, 3
Welch, Lieutenant George, 81
West Virginia, battleship, 64, 74, 75, 77, 82, 84, 96, 112, 115, 117
Wilhelm II, Kaiser, 2
"winds" message, 32

Yamaguchi, Rear Admiral Tamon, 46
Yamamoto, Admiral Isoroku, 11, 12, 23, 24, 27, 29, 30, 31, 35, 46, 48, 61, 88, 92, 103, 106, 107, 108, 118, 119
Yardley, Herbert O., 37
Yarnell, Admiral H. E., 21, 22
Yorktown, carrier, 26
Yoshikawa, Takeo AKA Morimura, Tadashi, 42, 118
Young, Commander Cassin, 68

Zaibatsu, 7
Zuikaku, carrier, 46, 47, 63